Investing in Real Estate Using Self-Directed Retirement Accounts

Written By

Ken Holman,

CCIM, CPM, CCA, CRS

In Conjunction with the

National Association of Real Estate Advisors (NAREA)

*for use in its **Certified Commercial Advisor (CCA)***

Designation Series

INVESTING IN REAL ESTATE USING SELF-DIRECTED RETIREMENT ACCOUNTS
© 2018 National Association of Real Estate Advisors, Inc. (NAREA)
Published by Realfacts, Inc.
14034 S. 145 E., Suite 100
Draper, Utah 84020
(866) 422-4200

ISBN: 978-1-947876-11-8

Kenneth T. Holman

Kenneth T. Holman founded the National Association of Real Estate Advisors (NAREA) in 2012. NAREA is an association that provides educational classes to real estate professionals.

Mr. Holman is also president of Overland Group, Inc., a multi-faceted real estate organization that provides, through its independently-owned and operated companies, brokerage, construction, development, financing, property management and real estate investing for its clients in both commercial and residential real estate.

Mr. Holman holds a Bachelor of Science degree in Accounting from Brigham Young University's Marriott School of Management and a Master of Business Administration (MBA) degree from the University of Utah's David Eccles School of Business.

Mr. Holman is past president of the Utah Apartment Association and has been a member of the Centerville City Council, a member of the Davis School District Foundation Board, and a founding member of the Centerville-Farmington Rotary Club.

Mr. Holman holds the following licenses: Real Estate Broker's License and General Contractor's License. He is affiliated with the following organizations and holds the following designations: CCIM (Certified Commercial Investment Member) with the CCIM Institute; CPM (Certified Property Manager) with the Institute of Real Estate Management (IREM); CCA (Certified Commercial Advisor) and REIA (Real Estate Investment Advisor) with the National Association of Real Estate Advisors; CRS (Certified Residential Specialist) with the Council of Residential Specialists; SRES (Seniors Real Estate Specialist) with the National Association of Realtors; and CDEI (Certified Distance Education Instructor) with the International Distance Education Certification Center (IDECC).

Mr. Holman can be reached at ken@nareagroup.org or by calling 801-931-5571.

National Association of Real Estate Advisors (NAREA)
Certified Commercial Advisor (CCA) Designation Requirements

COURSE #	REQUIRED COURSES	HOURS
101	Introduction to Commercial Real Estate Brokerage	3
102	Listing & Selling Commercial Real Estate	3
103	Leasing Commercial Real Estate	3
104	Marketing Commercial Real Estate	3
105	Financing Commercial Real Estate	3
106	Valuing Commercial Real Estate	3
107	Accounting & Taxation of Commercial Real Estate	3
108	Financial Analysis of Commercial Real Estate	3
109	Commercial Real Estate Contracts & Forms	3
110	Managing Commercial Real Estate	3
111	Investment Analysis of Commercial Real Estate	3
112	Investing in Real Estate Using Self-Directed Retirement Accounts	3
	TOTAL	36
	ELECTIVE COURSES (4 of 8 required)	
201	Brokering Multifamily Properties	3
202	Brokering & Leasing Retail Properties	3
203	Brokering & Leasing Office Properties	3
204	Brokering & Leasing Industrial Properties	3
205	Acquiring, Developing & Brokering Land	3
206	Preparing a Commercial Real Estate Feasibility Study	3
207	Brokering Lodging & Hospitality Properties	3
208	Brokering Investment Properties	3
	TOTAL	24
	GRAND TOTAL	60

About NAREA

NAREA Mission Statement

The National Association of Real Estate Advisors (NAREA) provides exceptional education to real estate professionals through its designation programs.

NAREA Designation Program

NAREA currently offers the following designation program: Certified Commercial Advisor (CCA).

A **Certified Commercial Advisor (CCA)** is a real estate professional who has demonstrated the ability to broker and lease commercial real estate. The CCA program requires a CCA Candidate to complete and pass, with 70 percent comprehension, a series of 12, 3-hour required courses. The CCA Candidate must also either demonstrate that they have completed three commercial transactions within a 12-month period prior to receiving the designation or they must complete 4 additional 3-hour elective courses.

NAREA Benefits

NAREA's website (www.nareagroup.org) offers many benefits and tools to assist both Candidates and Members. In addition to receiving the Certified Commercial Advisor (CCA) designation, other benefits include: Access to Online Courses; Sample Commercial Contracts and Forms; Financial and Investment Analysis Tools; Access to Books and Reports Available for Purchase and Use; a Monthly Newsletter and a Member Blog.

Table of Contents

Section One
Financial Planning

Objectives

- **To understand the role a financial planner plays in retirement planning**
- **To demonstrate the part real estate can play in asset allocation and diversification**
- **To state the importance of planning for retirement**

Financial Planning

Financial planning is the development and implementation of a coordinated plan for the achievement of financial objectives. A good financial plan addresses four questions:

- Where am I now?
- Where do I want to be in the future?
- How do I get to where I want to be?
- What action must I take to get where I want to be?

Assessing where you are right now requires analyzing one's current cash flow situation to determine how much money is coming in and where that money is being disbursed. It requires preparing a personal balance sheet and cash flow statement.

To determine where you want to be in the future requires establishing some long-term objectives, both financial and personal. Once long-term financial objectives have been established, it's time to develop an investment strategy to accumulate income-producing assets with a minimal amount of risk. After developing an appropriate investment strategy, it's time to take action.

A Financial Planner

Many people call themselves financial planners without having any credentials to prove they actually have the expertise to advise their clients. The most recognized financial planning designation is that of a Certified Financial Planner. A Certified Financial Planner (CFP) helps their clients pull their finances together, solve financial problems and make a plan to achieve their financial goals. Many financial planners form an alliance with a stock brokerage firm and/or an insurance company. These companies pay the CFP a commission for exclusively selling its products to their clients. This obviously biased conflict of interest leaves little room for real estate investments to be a part of a sound financial plan.

Financial planners use the "25 Times Rule" to help determine how much one's portfolio should be worth to safely retire. For instance, if you need $50,000 a year to live on when you retire, you should have $1,250,000 in stocks, bonds and mutual funds. Then, at retirement, the financial planner or stockbroker will begin liquidating those assets using the "4-Percent Rule," which simply means they liquidate 4 percent of your portfolio each year until you are down to zero after 25 years, hoping that if you retired at 65 you don't live past 90 or you're broke.

Tax-Deferred and Tax-Free Accounts

All those involved with financial planning must stress the importance of saving money for retirement in a tax-deferred or tax-free retirement account. The primary benefit of such an account is illustrated in the following graph that depicts an investment of $5,000 per year with one account earning interest at 10 percent for 30 years without the payment of taxes and one account earning interest at 10 percent for 30 years with the payment of taxes at 25 percent.

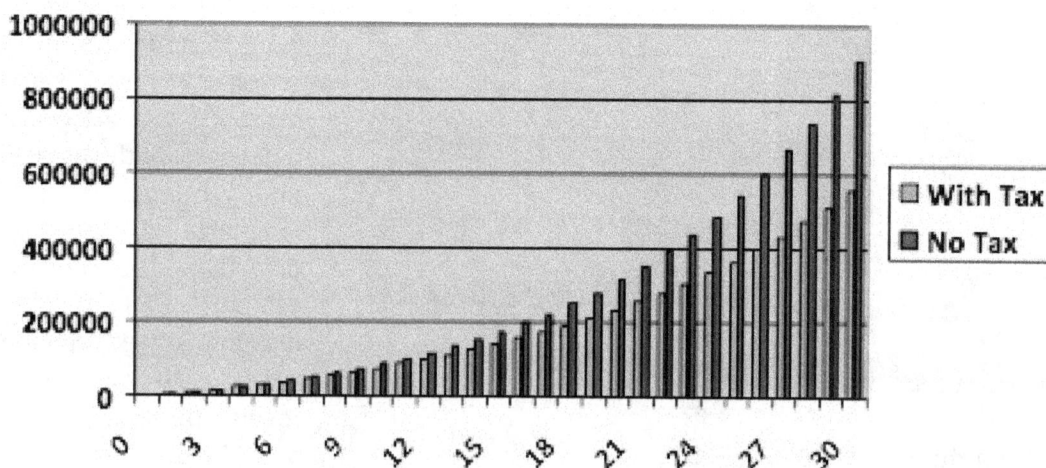

If a person invests $5,000 per year for 30 years earning interest at 10 percent, after 30 years, $150,000 has been invested. The interest earned on a tax-free or tax-deferred basis is $754,717 for a total of $904,717. When taxed at 25 percent, the principal invested is the same, but the interest earned declines to $405,772 for a total of $555,772. The tax impact on the sum earned is a loss of $348,945.

The Stock Market

Since 1929, the stock market has experienced numerous crashes and bear markets. During the latest economic downturn, the market experienced "high volatility and some gut-wrenching plunges." Many individual investors have left the market because of the perceived risk. Fear has caused many individual investors to pull back. One commentator likened the exodus of individual investors from the market as "rats fleeing from a sinking ship." Still reports show the largest portion of retirement plans continue to be invested in stocks. While the percentage of retirement plans invested in stocks has fallen over the years, there are still 65 percent of retirement plans' assets in stocks. Another nine percent are invested in bonds and balanced funds (funds that combine a stock component with a bond component). The remaining 26 percent hold their funds in cash and other investments.

Common stock is purchased by individual and institutional investors. Investor surveys place the number of individual shareholders at more than 50 million. The average stockholder has an average annual household income in the mid-$40,000 range and has around $10,000 invested, primarily through an Individual Retirement Account (IRA). Institutional buyers invest on behalf of individuals through pensions, trusts, profit-sharing, and mutual funds. Over the past three decades, institutional investors have come to dominate the market. They are the most important factor in the stock market today. They hold the majority of market value in the NYSE and most other exchanges. The largest institutional investors, based on the market value of their holdings, are uninsured pension funds, investment firms, nonprofit institutions, insurance companies, common trust funds, and mutual savings banks.

Mutual Funds

Mutual funds are investment vehicles that pool money from individual investors to increase their buying power and diversify their holdings. This allows investors to hold a number of securities in a single fund. There are two types of mutual funds: actively managed funds and index funds. An actively managed fund is managed by a professional money manager who handpicks investments according to the mutual fund's stated objectives. An index fund is not actively managed, but seeks to replicate the holdings of a specific index like the S&P 500.

One of the advantages of mutual funds is their diversification. The more stocks a mutual fund owns, the less impact on the portfolio if one of them tanks. Nearly as many mutual funds (more than 8,800) exist today as there are common stocks. All together, they comprise a staggering $7 trillion in assets. Unfortunately, when it comes to annual returns, 75 percent of them fail to beat the benchmark S&P 500 index.

Dalbar, Inc., a leading research company for the securities industry, in a study conducted in 2011, found the average equity mutual fund investor averaged a return of 3.27 percent over a 20-year period.

Bonds

Bonds are commonly referred to as fixed-income securities. Bonds are issued by companies, municipalities, states, the federal government, and foreign governments to borrow money from investors. An investor buys a bond, which, in effect, is a loan to the borrower. The credit quality of the borrowing entity and the duration of the bond determine its value. Most bonds have a face amount of $1,000. Each bond has a stated interest which the holder of the bond receives in periodic payments. Since the interest rate is fixed, as rates move up and down due to the economy, the price for which the bonds are bought and sold fluctuate to match current market conditions. If the stated interest rate on the bond is higher than the market rate, the bond is sold at a premium (more than $1,000). If the stated interest rate on the bond is lower than the current market rate, the bond is sold at a discount (lower than $1,000). Bonds are complex, especially for a novice investor with little experience in the markets.

The Lost Decade

Real estate has many advantages over investing in mutual funds. Real estate offers predictable cash flow, it appreciates in value, thus keeping up with inflation, it provides a higher return because of positive leverage, and it offers equity growth through debt reduction.

From 2001 to 2010, the stock market experienced what is now termed *The Lost Decade*. During this time, the Dow Jones Industrial Average started at about 11,600 and dropped 40 percent over the next three years. It took four years to get back to 11,600. In 2008, it dropped another 40 percent in one year and took another two years to get back to 11,600. After 10 years, the stock market ended where it began a decade earlier.

Asset Allocation

Asset allocation is an investment strategy that attempts to balance risk versus reward by adjusting the percentage of each asset in an investment portfolio according to the investor's risk tolerance, goals, and investment time frame. Asset allocation is based on the principle that different assets perform disparately in varying market and economic conditions.

Diversification

Similar to the concept of asset allocation, diversification is an investment strategy used to reduce risk by combining a variety of investments, such as stocks, bonds, and real estate, which are unlikely to all move in the same direction at the same time. Diversification tends to reduce volatility, but it also reduces both the upside and the downside potential and allows for a more consistent performance under a wide range of economic conditions.

Asset Allocation Chart

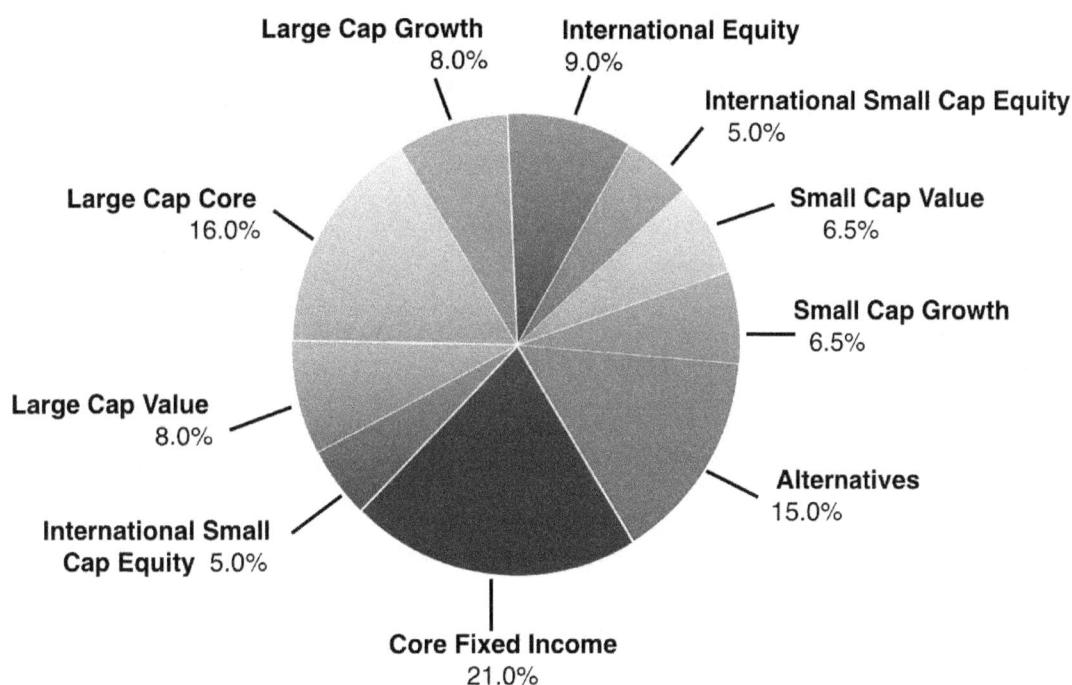

Large Cap Growth
8.0%

International Equity
9.0%

International Small Cap Equity
5.0%

Large Cap Core
16.0%

Small Cap Value
6.5%

Small Cap Growth
6.5%

Large Cap Value
8.0%

Alternatives
15.0%

International Small Cap Equity 5.0%

Core Fixed Income
21.0%

Asset Allocation and Diversification with Real Estate

The majority of investment capital is allocated among various stock investments, which creates tremendous volatility. A better investment strategy is to establish a strong foundation of income-producing real estate investments, which reduce risk and minimize volatility. The illustration on the following page is a better investment strategy for diversifying risk and maximizing return on investment.

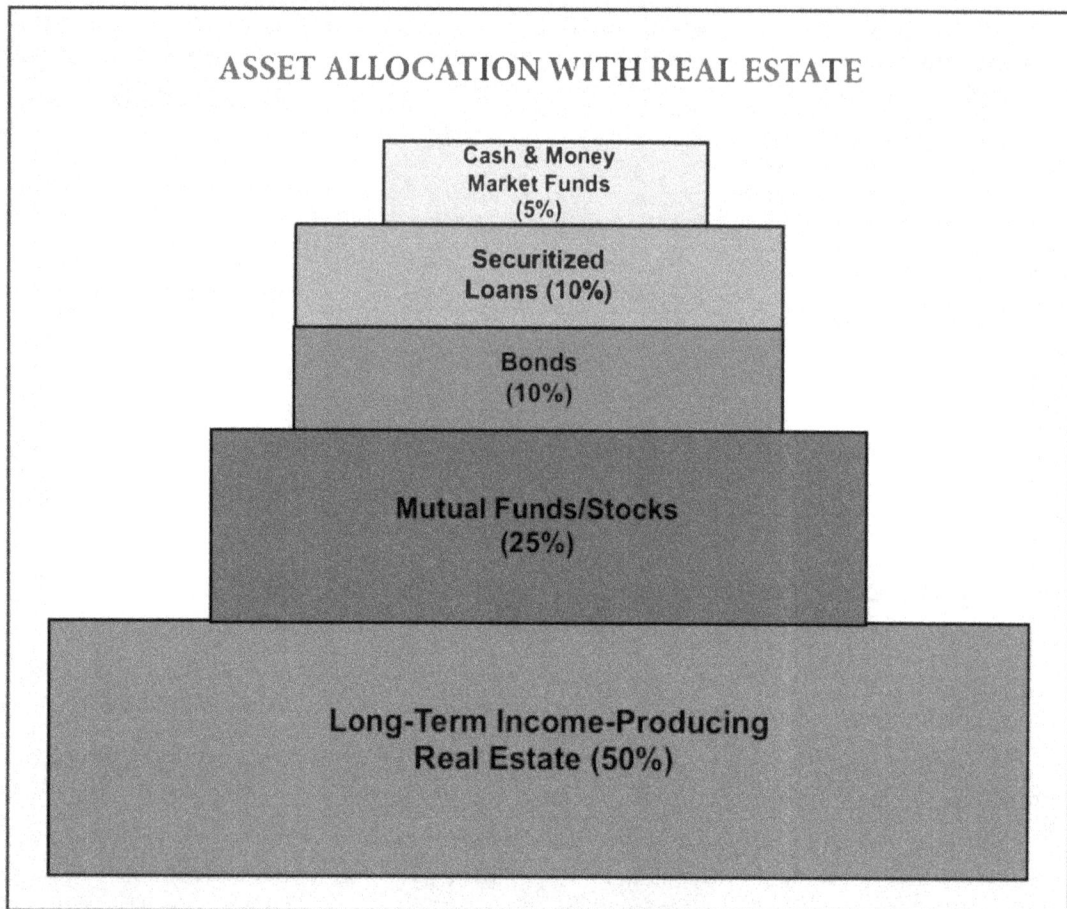

ASSET ALLOCATION WITH REAL ESTATE

Cash & Money
Market Funds
(5%)

Securitized
Loans (10%)

Bonds
(10%)

Mutual Funds/Stocks
(25%)

Long-Term Income-Producing
Real Estate (50%)

Retirement

People retire for the following reasons: they have accumulated enough financial resources to support themselves; they have reached the age of eligibility for retirement benefits; they are forced to retire due to physical conditions; or they have reached the mandatory retirement age set by their employer.

For most countries, early retirement begins between the ages of 55 and 60. The normal retirement age is between 65 and 67. For the United States, age 62 is considered early retirement, and age 67 is considered normal retirement age.

Have you thought about what you want to do during retirement? The way you spend your retirement years will determine how much income is needed. The following statistics depict how people want to spend their retirement years:

Travel the world	**19.6%**
Pursue creative passions	**16.7%**
Give back by volunteering	**11.3%**

Start a second career	**11.2%**
Sit home with my feet up	**10.1%**
Keep working (I need the money)	**9.1%**
Spoil the grandkids	**4.2%**
Launch my own business	**3.6%**
Keep working (I love my job)	**3.4%**
Go back to school	**2.1%**
Other	**8.7%**

Retirement Facts

- *USA Today* reports that out of 100 people age 65, 97 of them can't write a check for $600. Fifty four are still working, and three are financially secure.
- Bankruptcies among those 65 and older have gone up 164 percent in the last eight years.
- Baby boomers are reaching age 50 at a rate of more than 12,000 a day--one person every eight seconds. Today, more than 35 million Americans are over the age of 65. By 2025, that number will nearly double. Unfortunately, most do not have sufficient income to retire.
- Social Security will only provide about 40 percent of a person's retirement income. The other 60 percent must come from personal and retirement investments.
- People are living longer. When a man reaches age 65, his life expectancy is another 16.3 years. A woman's is another 19.2 years.
- Social Security has for many years been a system of transfer payments paid out of the general tax revenues. There is no trust fund, no shoebox in Baltimore with your money inside. The deduction from your paycheck this week will pay for a retiree's check next month.
- *The Wall Street Journal* reported that 70 percent of Americans live paycheck to paycheck.
- *Parenting Magazine* said 49 percent of Americans could cover less than one month's expenses if they lost their income.
- *USA Today* reported that 56 percent of Americans do not systematically prepare for retirement by investing.
- *Wealth Builder* Magazine's poll found that 80 percent of Americans believe their standard of living will go up when they retire.

People who do not save for their retirement and who do not invest wisely will never have the opportunity to retire. "Getting older is going to happen! You must invest now if you want to spend your golden years in dignity. Investing with the long-term goal of security is not a theory to ponder every few years; it is a necessity you must act on now." (Dave Ramsey, *Total Money Makeover*)

Planning for Retirement

The ratio of Social Security beneficiaries to the number of workers contributing to Social Security has dramatically increased, making it more difficult for the government to pay benefits. In 1940, 35.3 million workers were paying into the system with only 222,000 beneficiaries--a ratio of 159 to 1. By 2003, the number of workers had increased to 154.3 million, with 46.8 million beneficiaries--a ratio of 3.3 to 1. Medical costs have risen dramatically making it more difficult to cover medical expenses. Finally, life expectancy has nearly doubled primarily due to medical advances.

Year	Life Expectancy at Birth		Average Remaining Life Expectancy for those Surviving to Age 65		People Age 100 or Older	Number of Americans Age 65 or Older
	Males	Females	Males	Females		
1900	46.3	48.3				3.0 million
1910	49.9	53.2				3.9 million
1920	55.5	57.4				4.9 million
1930	57.7	60.9				6.7 million
1940	61.6	65.9	77.7	79.7		9.0 million
1950	65.6	71.1	77.8	80.0		12.7 million
1960	66.6	73.1	77.8	80.8		17.2 million
1970	67.1	74.7	78.1	82.0		20.9 million
1980	70.0	77.4	79.1	83.3		26.1 million
1990	71.8	78.8	80.1	83.9	37,306	31.9 million
2000	74.1	79.3	81.0	84.0	50,454	34.9 million
2007	75.4	80.4	82.2	84.9		36.8 million
2010	75.5	81.4	82.7	85.3	53,364	40.3 million
2050	81.2	86.6	90.9	93.3	834,000 mid-range	86.7 million

Source: National Vital Statistics System, Social Security Administration, New American Foundation, CDC, Census

Those living in the United States who follow sound financial management principles have an opportunity to acquire enough personal income-producing assets to retire comfortably, if not wealthy. Real estate is one of the best investments available to provide income before and during retirement. Accumulating income-producing assets is not easy. A person must follow some investment principles and have the discipline to set aside some hard-earned money for the future.

How many years will you spend in retirement? Based on average life expectancies, most financial planners assume people will live to age 85.

Life Expectancy			
Male		**Female**	
Age	**Life Expectancy**	**Age**	**Life Expectancy**
50	28	50	32
55	25	55	28
60	20	60	24
65	17	65	20
70	13	70	16
75	10	75	12
80	8	80	9
85	5	85	7
90	4	90	5
95	3	95	3
100	2	100	2
Source: Social Security Administration (www.ssa.gov), Period Life Table, 2013			

A man age 65 can expect to live another 17 years or to age 82, while a 65 year-old woman can expect to live another 20 years or to age 85. Because of advances in medicine and nutrition, people are living longer. In 2010, about 79,000 people will be over the age of 100, which was twice the number of a decade earlier. By 2050, that number is expected to top 1 million people in the United States.

Review Questions

1. Financial planning is the development and implementation of a coordinated plan for the achievement of financial objectives.

    A. True
    B. False

2. A good financial plan should address all of the following questions except:

    A. Where am I now?
    B. Where do I want to be in the future?
    C. What color should I paint the living room?
    D. What action must I take now to get to where I want to be?

3. Financial planners use the "25 Times Rule" to help determine how much one's portfolio should be worth to safely retire. Which of the following would be an example of the "25 Times Rule?"

    A. $50,000 Income x 20 Years = $1,000,000 at Retirement
    B. $50,000 Income x 25 Years = $1,250,000 at Retirement
    C. $25,000 Income x 20 Years = $500,000 at Retirement
    D. $100,000 Income x 10 Years = $1,000,000 at Retirement

4. Financial planners begin liquidating assets at retirement using the "4 Percent Rule." Which of the following would be an example of the "4 Percent Rule?"

    A. $1,000,000 at Retirement x 5% = $50,000 per year
    B. $1,250,000 at Retirement x 4% = $50,000 per year
    C. $500,000 at Retirement x 10% = $50,000 per year
    D. $1,500,000 at Retirement x 3.33% = $50,000 per year

5. If a person has $1,000,000 in a tax-deferred retirement account and decides to withdraw all of the money in one lump sum at retirement, how much will he/she pay in taxes if they are in a 25% tax bracket?

    A. $250,000
    B. $500,000
    C. $100,000
    D. Can't be determined from the information given

6. If a person has $1,000,000 in a tax-free retirement account and decides to withdraw all of the money in one lump sum at retirement, how much will he/she pay in taxes if they are in a 25% tax bracket?

    A. $250,000
    B. $500,000
    C. $100,000
    D. $0

7. The stock market is not a volatile industry and has seldom experienced crashes and bear markets since 1929.

    A. True
    B. False

8. From 2001 to 2010, the stock market experienced a situation where the Dow Jones Industrial Average began 2001 around 11,600 and ended in 2010 around 11,600. That period of time in stock market history has been referred to as _____?

    A. The Forgotten Decade
    B. The Non-Performing Decade
    C. The Lost Decade
    D. The Disappoint Decade

9. An attempt to balance risk versus reward by adjusting the percentage of each asset in an investment portfolio according to an investor's risk tolerance, goals, and investment time frame is called:

    A. Asset Allocation
    B. Return Maximization
    C. Risk Tolerance
    D. Asset Diversification

10. An investment strategy used to reduce risk by combining a variety of investments, such as stocks, bonds, and real estate, which are unlikely to all move in the same direction at the same time is called:

    A. Asset Allocation
    B. Return Maximization
    C. Risk Tolerance
    D. Asset Diversification

11. Baby boomers are reaching age 50 at what approximate number each day?

    A. 4,000
    B. 8,000
    C. 12,000
    D. 20,000

12. The life expectancy for men and women over the next 30 years is expected to:

    A. Increase
    B. Decrease
    C. Remain the same

Section Two
Retirement Accounts

Objectives

- **To introduce retirement accounts**
- **To define pension plans, defined benefit plans and defined contribution plans**
- **To introduce 401(k) plans, one-participant 401(k) plans, 403(b) plans and 457 plans**

Retirement Accounts

A real estate professional can have both an Individual Retirement Account (IRA) and a 401(k) retirement account and can contribute to both simultaneously. One can also have more than one IRA account and more than one 401(k) account. However, a person can only contribute the maximum allowed by law regardless of how many accounts one has.

Types of Retirement Accounts

Retirement accounts are classified into two broad categories: Defined Benefit Plans and Defined Contribution Plans. As the names imply, one category relates to the benefit received from an employer, and the other category relates to the contribution made as an employee. Most companies and organizations offer either a Defined Benefit Plan or a Defined Contribution Plan, but not both.

Before 1978, Defined Benefit Pension Plans were the predominant retirement program available to employees. The government and other public institutions, as well as labor unions and many large corporations, established Defined Benefit Pension Plans, usually called Pension Plans, to attract employees and to provide benefits at retirement. Many pension plans have had slow earnings growth due to bad fund managers, slow economic times, and an increasing life expectancy rate. These severe shortages require some companies to take out bankruptcy to avoid paying retired employees their promised benefits.

In 1978, Defined Contribution Plans came into existence, which shifted the responsibility of contributing to a retirement plan from the employer to the employee. Now many major companies have Defined Contribution Plans rather than Defined Benefit Plans.

Defined Benefit Plans

A Defined Benefit Pension Plan or Defined Benefit Plan is a type of retirement plan where the employer or sponsor promises to pay a specified monthly benefit to the employee upon retirement. The amount paid to the employee is based on a formula that takes into consideration the employee's earnings history, his tenure of service, and his age.

Traditionally, many governmental and public entities, as well as large corporations, provided Defined Benefit Plans. In the private sector, Defined Benefit Plans are often funded entirely by employer contributions. Over time, many of these plans have faced significant deficits.

Pension Plans

A pension is merely a fixed sum paid to an employee upon retirement. The term pension refers to both Defined Benefit Plans and Defined Contribution Plans.

Defined Contribution Plans

A Defined Contribution Plan is a type of retirement plan in which the employee and sometimes the employer, by matching the employee's contributions up to a certain percentage, make regular contributions to an account for the benefit of the employee. These contributions are then invested, usually in the stock market, on behalf of the employee.

Most Defined Contribution Plans are simply named based on the section of the Internal Revenue Code (IRC) in which they are found. The three most common are 401(k), 403(b) and 457. Pension plans, 401(k) and 403(b) plans are considered qualified plans. The 457 plan is a nonqualified plan; however, all of the plans receive favorable tax treatment, especially the 457 plan.

401(k) Plans

The Revenue Act of 1978 became Internal Revenue Code (IRC) Section 401(k). This Act allowed employees to defer a part of their compensation from tax liability by contributing to a deferred arrangement plan. One of the earliest companies to adopt the 401(k) plan was Hughes Aircraft Company, which adopted the 401(k) plan as a standard retirement saving arrangement.

By 1983, almost half of all major employers in America had switched from offering pension plans to offering 401(k) plans. By 1984, more than 17,303 plans covered 7.54 million active participants with a total combined amount of $91.75 billion.

A 401(k) plan is a qualified profit-sharing, stock bonus, pre-ERISA money purchase pension under which an employee can elect to have the employer contribute a portion of the employee's cash wages to the plan on a pre-tax basis. These deferred wages (indexed annually for inflation at $500 increments) are not subject to Federal income tax withholding at the time of the deferral. They are not reflected as taxable income on Form 1040 U.S. Individual Income Tax Return. Although these elective deferrals are not treated as current income for Federal income tax purposes, they are included as wages subject to social security (FICA), Medicare, and Federal Unemployment Taxes (FUTA). (*Refer to Publication 525*).

Two of the advantages of participating in a 401(k) plan are elective deferrals and investment gains are not subject to federal income taxes until distributed from the plan, and elective deferrals are always 100 percent vested.

Contribution Limits in a One-Participant 401(k) Plan

The business owner is an employee and employer in a 401 (k) plan. Contributions can be made to the plan in both capacities. The owner can contribute both:

- Elective deferrals up to 100 percent of compensation (Earned income in the case of a self-employed individual) up to the annual contribution limit, which in 2017 is $18,000 if under the age of 50 and $24,000 (includes the $6,000 catch-up contribution) if age 50 or older.
- Employer non-elective contributions up to 25 percent of compensation as defined by the plan, or for self-employed individuals, net earnings from self-employment after deducting both one-half of self-employment tax and contributions to one's self.

Example: Ben, age 51, earned $100,000 in W-2 wages from his S Corporation in 2017. He deferred $18,000 in regular elective deferrals plus $6,000 in catch-up contributions to the 401(k) plan. His business contributed 25 percent ($25,000) of his compensation to the plan. Total contributions to the plan for 2017 were $49,000 ($18,000 + $6,000 + $25,000 = $49,000). Ben could actually contribute $54,000 to the plan if his earned income were $120,000 ($18,000 regular elective deferral plus $6,000 in catch-up contributions plus 25 percent of $120,000 or $30,000 for a total of $54,000). It should also be noted in this example that the employee regular elective deferral plus the catch-up contribution could be made by the employee as either a Traditional (pre-tax) contribution or as a Roth (post-tax) contribution, however, the 25 percent contributed by the company would always be considered a Traditional (pre-tax) contribution because the company can expense the company contribution on its books and the employee does not recognize the income at the time the contribution is made.

A business owner who is also employed by a second company and participating in its 401(k) plan should bear in mind that the limits on elective deferrals are by person, not by plan. A one-participant 401(k) plan is generally required to file an annual report on Form 5500-SF if it has $250,000 or more in assets at the end of the year. A one-participant plan with fewer assets may be exempt from the annual filing requirement.

Matching Contributions: If the plan document permits, the employer can make matching contributions for an employee who contributes elective deferrals to the 401(k) plan. For example, a 401(k) plan might provide that the employer will contribute 50 cents for each dollar that participating employees choose to defer under the plan usually up to a certain limit.

One-Participant 401(k) Plans: The one-participant 401(k) plan is a traditional 401(k) plan covering a business owner with no employees, or that person and his or her spouse. These plans are sometimes called a Solo-k, Solo-401(k), Individual (k), Uni-k, or One-participant k and have the same rules and requirements as any other 401(k) plan.

403(b) Plans

A 403(b) Plan is primarily for certain employees of tax-exempt 501(c)(3) organizations such as public schools, public hospitals, and certain ministers. The features of a 403(b) plan are similar to those of a 401(k) plan where employees make salary deferral contributions that are based on certain regulatory requirements. (*The following information is taken verbatim from the IRS's website www.irs.gov/Retirement-Plans.*)

Generally, contributions to an employee's 403(b) account are limited to the lesser of the limit on annual additions or the elective deferral limit.

The limit on annual additions (the combination of all employer contributions and employee elective deferrals to all 403(b) accounts) generally is the lesser of $54,000 for 2017, or 100 percent of includible compensation for the employee's most recent year of service. Generally, includible compensation is the amount of taxable wages and benefits the employee received in the employee's most recent full year of service.

The limit on elective deferrals—the most an employee can contribute to a 403(b) account by means of a salary reduction agreement—is $18,000 in 2017.

457 Plans

The 457 plan is a type of non-qualified, tax advantaged, deferred-compensation retirement plan that is available for governmental and certain non-governmental employees in the United States. The employer provides the plan and the employee defers compensation into it on a pre-tax basis. For the most part, the plan operates similarly to a 401(k) or 403(b) plan, but the key difference is there is no 10 percent penalty for withdrawal before the age of 59½ (although the withdrawal is subject to ordinary income taxation). Also, 457 plans can allow for participation of independent contractors to the plan where 401(k) or 403(b) plans cannot. A 457 plan does not require the coordination of benefits limitation as do the other plans, meaning a person whose employer has a 401(k) or 403(b) plan and a 457 plan can contribute the maximum amount to both plans instead of only being able to meet a single limit amount.

Review Questions

1. A real estate professional can have both an Individual Retirement Account (IRA) and a 401(k) retirement account and can contribute to both simultaneously.

    A. True
    B. False

2. Retirement accounts can be classified into two broad categories. Select the choices that correspond to the correct answers.

    A. Defined Benefit Plans
    B. Defined Contribution Plans
    C. Both A and B
    D. Neither A nor B

3. A type of retirement plan where the employer or sponsor promises to pay a specified monthly benefit to the employee upon retirement is called:

    A. A Defined Contribution Plan
    B. A Defined Benefit Plan
    C. A 401(k) Plan
    D. An IRA Plan

4. A type of retirement plan in which the employee and sometimes the employer, by matching the employee's contributions up to a certain percentage, make regular contributions to an account for the benefit of the employee is known as:

    A. A Pension Plan
    B. A Defined Benefit Plan
    C. An Automatic Withdrawal Plan
    D. A Defined Contribution Plan

5. Which of the following retirement plans would be considered a Defined Benefit Plan?

    A. A Pension Plan
    B. A 401(k) Plan
    C. An IRA Plan
    D. A 403(b) Plan

6. Which of the following retirement plans would be considered a Defined Contribution Plan?

    A. A 401(k) Plan
    B. A 403(b) Plan
    C. A 457 Plan
    D. All of the above

7. Internal Revenue Code (IRC) Section 401(k) allowed employees to defer a part of their compensation from tax liability by contributing to a deferred arrangement plan. These plans are known as:

    A. 403(b) Plans
    B. 401(k) Plans
    C. IRA Plans
    D. Savings Plans

8. Which of the following is an advantage of a 401(k) plan?

    A. Deferred compensation is not taxed until distributed
    B. Investment gains are not taxed until distributed
    C. Both A and B above
    D. Neither A nor B above

9. A business owner can be both the employer and the sole employee in a company and have a 401(k) plan.

    A. True
    B. False

10. A 401(k) plan that has the business owner as its sole employee is known as:

    A. A One-participant 401(k) plan
    B. An Individual 401(k) plan
    C. A Solo 401(k) plan
    D. All of the above

11. A retirement plan that is primarily for certain employees of tax-exempt 501(c)(3) organizations such as public schools, public hospitals, and certain ministers is known as:

    A. A 401(k) Plan
    B. A 403(b) Plan
    C. A 457 Plan
    D. None of the above

12. A retirement plan in the United States that is available to governmental and certain non-governmental employees who work for the government is known as:

    A. A 401(k) Plan
    B. A 403(b) Plan
    C. A 457 Plan
    D. None of the above

Section Three
Individual Retirement Accounts

Objectives

- **To introduce individual retirement accounts**
- **To discuss the basic types of IRAs**
- **To explain the difference between Traditional and Roth IRAs**

Individual Retirement Accounts

Individual Retirement Accounts (IRA) provide investors the opportunity to save for retirement either on a tax-deferred or tax-free basis to enable their earnings to grow faster than traditional savings accounts where the interest is taxed at ordinary income tax rates. IRAs may be started by employees or by employers and have a variety of different structures and applications.

History of Individual Retirement Accounts

In 1974, the Employee Retirement Income Security Act (ERISA) was enacted. It established minimum standards for pension plans in private industry and set rules governing employee benefit plan participants. ERISA created the first individual retirement account which allowed tax deductible contributions of $1,500 per year. For the first few years, IRAs were limited to those who didn't have a work retirement plan.

In 1997, the Taxpayer Relief Act created both an Education IRA and what is known as a Roth IRA, which allows non-deductible contributions into an account which can be redeemed at a later date with no tax penalty and allows tax-free early withdrawals under certain conditions. This means that a Roth IRA never is taxed on the income it earns. Income thresholds were also raised, allowing those with higher incomes to deduct contributions, especially if they did not have a retirement account at work.

In 2001, the Economic Growth and Tax Relief Reconciliation Act (EGTRRA) increased the maximum contribution level and included a special catch-up clause for contributions for people ages 50 and over.

Basic Types of IRAs

Four types of IRAs exist. Two are specifically designed for employees of small businesses, and two are designed for individuals. Spousal IRAs and Rollover IRAs are variations on the two individual IRA programs.

SEP-IRA

A SEP-IRA (Simplified Employee Pension Individual Retirement Account) is a type of employer-provided IRA that allows business owners to provide retirement benefits for the business owners and their employees. This plan can be used for self-employed persons with or without any employees. If the self-employed person does have employees, all employees must receive the same benefits under the SEP-IRA plan. Since SEP accounts are treated as IRAs, funds can be invested in the same way that any other IRA may invest funds.

Requirements of a SEP-IRA	
The deadline for establishing a SEP-IRA and making contributions is the filing deadline for the employer's tax return, including any extensions.	
Employee eligibility conditions apply	• Must be at least 21 years of age • Must have worked for the employer for at least three of the previous five years • Must receive at least $500 in compensation for the tax year
When qualified withdrawals are taken after age 59½, the funds are taxed as ordinary income tax.	
Contributions to an SEP-IRA plan are deductible, which lowers the taxpayer's income tax liability for that year.	
SEP-IRA contributions are treated as part of a profit-sharing plan. For employees, the employer may contribute up to 25 percent of the employee's wages.	For example, if an employee earns $40,000 in wages, the employer may contribute up to $10,000 to the employee's SEP-IRA account.
The total contribution to an SEP-IRA account should not exceed the lesser of 25 percent of total salary or $54,000.	
Contributions may be made to the plan up to the date the employer's tax return is due for that year.	
The contribution limit for a self-employed person is somewhat complicated. It is approximately 18.6 percent of net profit adjusted for the deduction for self-employment tax.	The formula for the computation is found in IRS Publication 560, Section 5, entitled Table and Worksheets for the Self-Employed, specifically Deduction Worksheet for Self-Employed. Since the contribution limit for a self-employed person is complicated, it is advisable to seek competent advice from a qualified accountant.

SIMPLE IRA

A SIMPLE IRA (Savings Incentive Match Plan for Employees) is a type of employer-provided IRA that allows employees to set aside money and invest it on a tax-deferred basis. Like more well-known 401(k) profit-sharing plans, SIMPLE is funded with pretax salary deductions, but for the employer is simpler and less costly to administer. Contribution limits for SIMPLE plans are lower than most other types of employer-provided retirement plans. For 2017, the limit is $12,500 compared to $18,000 for 401(k) and 403(b) defined contribution plans. In 2017, for employees age 50 and older, the contribution limit for a SIMPLE IRA is $15,500, which includes the $3,000 catch-up contribution. For a 501(c)(3) non-profit employer, there is no advantage in establishing a SIMPLE plan over a 403(b) plan.

Requirements of a SIMPLE IRA
Only an eligible employer may establish a SIMPLE IRA. An eligible employer is one with no more than 100 employees.
The plan requires a minimum contribution from the employer. The employer may either match the contributions of the employees dollar-for-dollar up to three percent or the employer may contribute a flat two percent of compensation for each employee with at least $5,000 in compensation for the year, regardless of the amount the employee contributes.
Unlike a 401(k), a SIMPLE IRA cannot be rolled over to a Traditional IRA without a two-year waiting period from the date the employee first participated in the plan.
SEP IRAs and Traditional IRAs cannot be rolled over into a SIMPLE IRA.
If an employee wishes to take an early distribution from a SIMPLE IRA, there is a penalty fee assessed by the IRS of 25 percent of the entire distribution. Also, if the account holder is also under 59½ years of age, there is an additional penalty of 10 percent plus the standard income tax applies.

Traditional IRA

Traditional IRAs, originally called Regular IRAs, were created in 1975. A Traditional IRA is an individual retirement account. The only criterion for being eligible to contribute to a Traditional IRA is sufficient income to make the contribution. The contributions are tax deductible for the tax year in which the contribution was made, however, when qualified withdrawals occur, the income is taxed at ordinary income tax rates. During the life of a Traditional IRA, all income earned is allowed to grow tax-deferred until the time of the withdrawals. Combined Traditional and Roth IRA Contribution Limits for 2017 are:

1. If you are under 50 years of age at the end of 2017, the maximum contribution that can be made to a Traditional or Roth IRA is the lessor of $5,500 or the

amount of your taxable compensation for 2017. This limit can be split between a Traditional IRA and a Roth IRA but the combined limit is $5,500. The maximum deductible contribution to a Traditional IRA and the maximum contribution to a Roth IRA may be reduced depending on the Modified Adjusted Gross Income (MAGI). Consult a tax accountant to calculate MAGI.

2. If you are 50 years of age or older before the end of 2017, the maximum contribution that can be made to a Traditional or Roth IRA is the lessor of $6,500 or the amount of the taxable compensation for 2017. This limit can be split between a Traditional IRA and a Roth IRA but the combined limit is $6,500. The maximum deductible contribution to a Traditional IRA and the maximum contribution to a Roth IRA may be reduced depending on MAGI.

U.S. taxable compensation is necessary to use these accounts. Compensation is defined as wages, salaries, and alimony but not dividend, interest, or capital gain income. The money must be received during the same year as the contribution, although one can make the contributions as late as April 15 of the next year. This rule applies to all types of IRAs.

2017 Traditional & Roth IRA Contribution Limits			
Plan Name	**Standard Limit**	**Catch-Up Limit (Age 50 and Older)**	**Total**
Traditional	$5,500	$1,000	$6,500
Roth	$5,500	$1,000	$6,500
If you are covered by a plan at work, the following income limits apply (Modified AGI Limits for 2017): **Single: No limit if you are not covered by another retirement plan** **Married Filing Jointly: $186,000 or less** **2017 Traditional & Roth IRA Contribution Deadline is 4/15/2018**			

Traditional IRA Considerations
Even if a contribution cannot be deducted, a contribution can still be made. This is called a nondeductible IRA.
You can have as many different IRA accounts as you like, but the total contribution across all accounts (Traditional and Roth) for the year is still $5,500 per person, unless you are over 50 and then it's $6,500.
You must open the IRA at an institution approved by the IRS.
Although some exceptions are made, this account is for retirement and should not be touched until you are at least 59½, otherwise certain penalties apply.
If you withdraw the money early, the IRS will charge you not only the taxes that would normally be due on your withdrawal, but also an additional 10 percent as a penalty to discourage the withdrawal. Think twice before taking money out early.
The exceptions to avoid the additional 10 percent tax include: disability, death of the account holder, first-time homebuyers, health insurance premiums, healthcare expenses, education expenses, tax levies, or retired early and taking substantially equal payments (SEPP).
To claim one of these exceptions, you must have had the IRA at least five years, or the 10 percent penalty applies.
You cannot continue to contribute once you reach age 70½ years of age. In fact, beginning at age 70½, you have to start taking out Required Minimum Distributions (RMDs). For the first few years, the RMD is about four percent of the account, but by the time you reach 90, it is about 10 percent of the account value. Do not forget to take this out every year or you will pay a very stiff penalty; 50 percent of what you should have taken out will go to the IRS.
You cannot borrow money from an IRA. A withdrawal is a withdrawal—you must pay any applicable tax and penalties and you cannot pay it back later.

ROTH IRA

A Roth IRA is a special type of individual retirement account that is not taxed, provided certain conditions are met. The Roth IRA's principal difference from a Traditional IRA is that the contributions are not tax deductible, but the earnings in the account may be withdrawn tax free if certain qualifications are met.

Roth IRAs were originally called American Dream Savings Accounts but were later renamed after their chief advocate, Senator William Roth of Delaware.

"The Roth IRA is perhaps the greatest gift ever given to the American investor... Because of these very favorable rules, a Roth IRA should be one of the first places you put money for retirement and one of the last places you withdraw it from...When you combine the magic of compounding with tax-free growth and a healthy disinclination to spend, truly amazing things are possible." (Jim Dahle, *The Bogleheads' Guide to Retirement Planning*, p. 51).

A Roth IRA contribution is affected by the amount of Modified Adjusted Gross Income (MAGI) an owner makes. The table below shows the MAGI limits that determine whether or not an owner can make a contribution.

Filing Status	Modified AGI	Contribution
Married filing jointly or qualifying widow(er)	< $186,000	Up to the limit
	≥ $186,000 but < $196,000	A reduced amount
	≥ $196,000	Zero
Married filing separately and you lived with your spouse at any time during the year	< $10,000	A reduced amount
	≥ $10,000	Zero
Single, head of household, or married filing separately and you did not live with your spouse at any time during the year	< $118,000	Up to the limit
	≥ $118000 but < $133,000	A reduced amount
	≥ $133,000	Zero

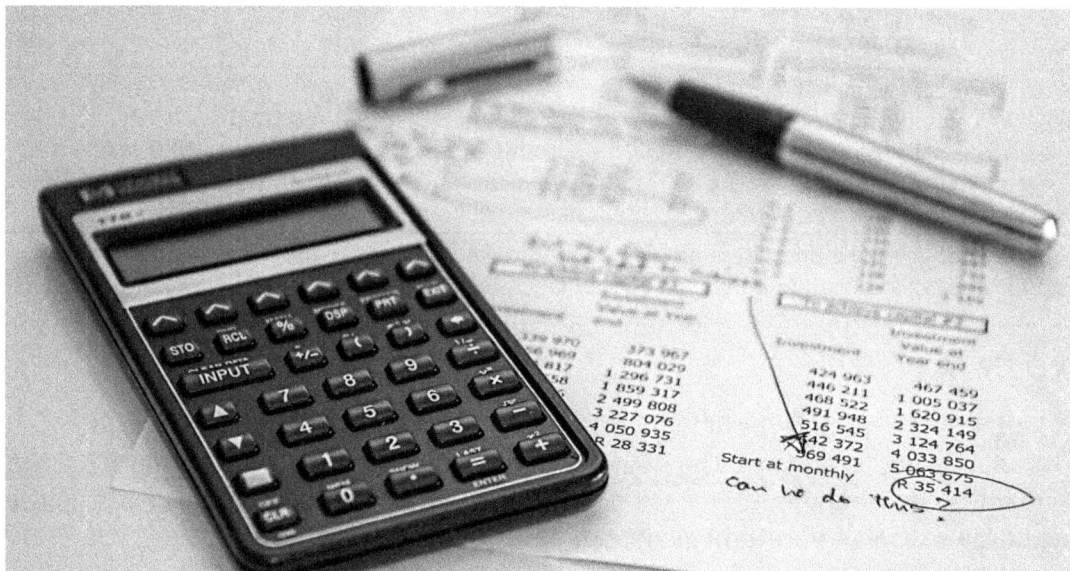

Roth IRA v. Traditional IRA

Some types of IRAs have an income limit. All IRAs have a contribution limit. These limits are variable because of changes in law or inflation. Check with the IRS or a tax adviser every year to stay up to date.

The Difference Between Traditional and Roth IRAs*		
Question	**Answer**	
	Traditional IRA	**Roth IRA**
Is there an age limit on when one can open and contribute?	Yes. You must not have reached age 70½ by the end of the year .	No. You can be any age.
Is there a limit on how much can be contributed each year?	Yes.	Yes, but the amount one can contribute may be less depending on income, filing status, and if contributing to another IRA.
Can contributions be deducted?	Yes. One may be able to deduct contributions to a Traditional IRA depending on income, filing status, whether they are covered by a retirement plan at work, and whether they receive social security benefits.	No. One can never deduct contributions to a Roth IRA.
Does one have to file a form just because they contributed?	Not unless you make nondeductible contributions to a Traditional IRA. In that case, one must file Form 8606.	No. One does not have to file a form if they contribute to a Roth IRA.
Does one have to start taking distributions when they reach a certain age?	es. They must begin receiving required minimum distributions by April 1 of the year following the year they	No. If they are the original owner of a Roth IRA, they do not have to take distributions regardless of their age.
How are distributions taxed?	Distributions from a traditional IRA are taxed as ordinary income, but if one made nondeductible contributions, not all of the distribution is	Distributions from a Roth IRA are not taxed as long as they meet certain criteria.
Does one have to file a form just because they receive distributions?	Not unless they have ever made a nondeductible contribution to a traditional IRA. If they have, file Form 8606.	Yes. File Form 8606 if they received distributions from a Roth IRA (other than a rollover, qualified charitable distribution, one-time distribution to fund an HSA, re-characterization, certain qualified distributions, or a return of certain contributions).

Remember to always discuss these matters with an accountant or tax consultant before making any major decisions.

Retirement Account Investing Strategies

TRADITIONAL	ROTH
Tax-Deferred	*Tax-Free*
IRA	
• Pre-Tax • UDFI Tax • Ordinary Income Tax • RMD @ 70 1/2	• After Tax • UDFI Tax • No Income Tax • No RMD
401(k)	
• Pre-Tax • No UDFI • Ordinary Income Tax • RMD @ 70 1/2 • Company Match • Profit Sharing	• After Tax • No UDFI • No Income Tax • RMD @ 70 1/2 • Only Applies to Contributions

Resources

IRS Publications for IRA and Small Business Plans	
IRS Publication 529	Miscellaneous Deductions
IRS Publication 550	Investment Income and Expenses
IRS Publication 560	Small Business Retirement Plans
IRS Publication 575	Pensions and Annuities
IRS Publication 590	Individual Retirement Accounts
IRS Publication 3125	Information on IRA approved investments
IRC Section 4925	Disqualified Persons

IRS Publications for Health Savings and Education Plans	
IRS Publication 502	Medical and Dental Expenses
IRS Publication 939	General Rule for Pensions and Annuities
IRS Publication 969	Health Savings Accounts and Other
IRS Publication 970	Tax Benefits for Higher Education

Review Questions

1. Individual Retirement Accounts (IRAs) provide investors the opportunity to save for retirement on either a tax-deferred or tax-free basis to enable their earnings to grow faster than traditional savings accounts where the interest is taxed at ordinary income tax rates at the time that it is earned.

   A. True
   B. False

2. In 1974, ERISA was enacted to establish minimum standards for pension plans in private industry and set rules for governing employee benefit plan participants. ERISA created the first individual retirement account. What does the acronym ERISA stand for?

   A. Employer Retirement Investment Securities Act
   B. Employee Retirement Income Security Act
   C. Essential Retirement Investment Securities Act
   D. Employee Real Interesting Social Act

3. Which of the following is NOT a type of Individual Retirement Account (IRA)?

   A. SEP-IRA
   B. SIMPLE IRA
   C. Traditional IRA
   D. 401(k)

4. The Simplified Employee Pension Individual Retirement Account is a type of employer-provided IRA that allows business owners to provide retirement benefits for the business owners and their employees. What is the acronym for the above-mentioned account?

   A. SIMPLE IRA
   B. SEP-IRA
   C. ROTH IRA
   D. Traditional IRA

5. The Savings Incentive Match Plan for Employees is a type of employer-provided IRA that allows employees to set aside money and invest on a tax-deferred basis. What is the acronym for the above-mentioned plan?

   A. SIMPLE IRA
   B. SEP-IRA
   C. ROTH IRA
   D. Traditional IRA

6. In a Traditional IRA, the contributions are tax deductible for the year in which the contribution was made.

   A. True
   B. False

7. In 2017, if you were under 50 years of age, the maximum amount you could contribute to a Traditional or Roth IRA was:

   A. $4,000
   B. $4,500
   C. $5,000
   D. $5,500

8. In 2017, if you were 50 years of age or older, the maximum amount you could contribute to a Traditional or Roth IRA based on the Catch-Up contribution was:

   A. $5,000
   B. $5,500
   C. $6,000
   D. $6,500

9. A Roth IRA is a special type of Individual Retirement Account named after Senator William Roth of Delaware. One of the principal differences between a Traditional IRA and a Roth IRA is:

   A. The contributions are tax deductible
   B. The contributions are not tax deductible
   C. There is no difference between a Traditional IRA and a Roth IRA

10. A Roth IRA is a special type of Individual Retirement Account. One of the principal differences between a Traditional IRA and a Roth IRA is:

   A. The earnings in the account may NOT be withdrawn tax free
   B. The earnings in the account may be withdrawn tax free
   C. There are no differences between the Traditional IRA and the Roth IRA

11. If you have a Traditional IRA, what is the age limit on when you can contribute?

   A. 65
   B. 70 ½
   C. 75
   D. There is no age limit

12. If you have a Roth IRA, what is the age limit on when you can contribute?

   A. 65
   B. 70 ½
   C. 75
   D. There is no age limit

Section Four
Self-Directed Retirement Accounts

Objectives

- **To introduce self-directed retirement accounts**
- **To explain why an individual 401(k) is better than an IRA**
- **To discuss permitted and prohibited transactions**

Self-Directed Retirement Accounts

A self-directed retirement account is technically no different than any other IRA except it allows the account owner to invest in other types of investments. Both IRA and 401(k) retirement accounts can be self-directed. A self-directed individual retirement account is either a Traditional or a Roth IRA that has been set up to allow the account owner to select a variety of investments for the benefit of the retirement plan. Self-directed retirement accounts may be invested in stocks, bonds and mutual funds, but are not limited strictly to those asset types. A self-directed retirement account may also be invested in a number of other IRS permitted investment types, such as real estate, mortgages, franchises, partnerships, private equity and tax liens. IRS regulations require that either a qualified trustee or custodian hold the IRA assets on behalf of the IRA owner.

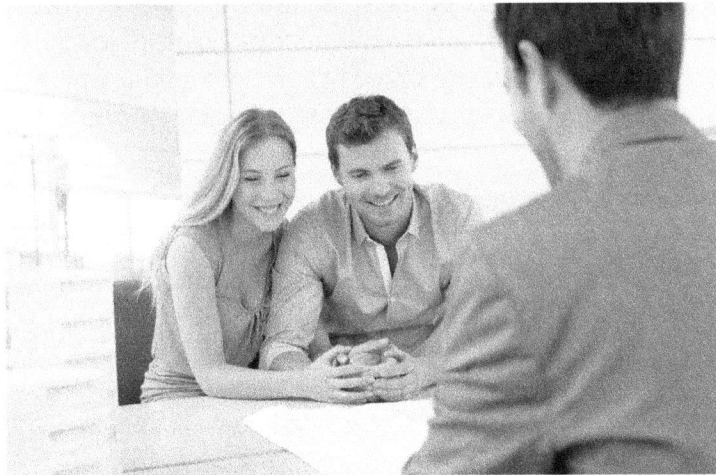

Most banks, stock brokerages, insurance companies, and financial planners and/or advisors who are affiliated with an independent broker-dealer will not permit the IRAs they manage to be self- directed. They require their clients to select investments from the products they offer for sale. A self-directed retirement account gives more investment choices than the typical situation.

An Individual 401(k) Account is Better Than an IRA

What is a Self-Directed Individual 401(k) Account?

The term self-directed refers to any retirement account where the owner of the account personally directs where the retirement funds are to be invested. Self-directed 401(k) retirement accounts are similar to any other type of 401(k) account. They derive their name from Section 401 of the Internal Revenue Code.

These 401(k) qualified retirement plans came into being in 1974 with the passage of the Employee Retirement Income Security act (ERISA), however, individual 401(k) accounts didn't become permanent until 2002 with the passage of the Economic Growth and Tax Relief Act of 2001 (EGTRRA), commonly known as the Bush Tax Cuts.

The Internal Revenue Service (IRS) refers to these types of accounts as one-participant 401(k) plans. Some 401(k) administrators have called these one-participant 401(k) plans by other names, e.g., Individual (k), Solo 401(k), Solo-k, and Uni-k. These are different names for the same plan. I have chosen to use the term Individual K to refer to all one-participant plans.

Individual 401(k) plans are designed specifically for businesses that employ only the owner and/or their spouse or their partners. They have no other employees. These plans are perfectly suited for sole practitioners like self-employed consultants, real estate professionals, sales people, private contractors, sole proprietors and any person who does not control the company they work for and who want to start a consulting business on the side.

If you are a 1099 independent contractor, it is likely you would be a good candidate for a Self-Directed Individual 401(k). The term 1099 refers to the IRS form that an independent contractor receives from a company stating his/her income that was paid for activity or service that was performed.

Benefits of a Self-Directed Individual 401(k) Account

There are basically two individual 401(k) account options available: the brokerage-directed account and the self-directed account. Brokerage-based plans are established through a stockbroker, a banker or financial planner. These plans limit the investment choices to market-based assets such as individual stocks and mutual funds that are sold by the firm with whom the adviser is affiliated.

Self-directed plans, on the other hand, are established with an IRS-approved independent third party administrator who handles administration of the qualified plan and is affiliated with a federally-insured custodian to safeguard your retirement funds until the account owner decides which investments are suitable for his/her plan. A self-directed individual 401(k) plan is the most tax-advantaged plan available among the various retirement plan options.

41

The benefits and advantages of having a Self-directed Individual 401(k) plan are significant.

1. The contribution limits to a Self-directed Individual 401(k) are the same as a standard 401(k). Contributions are separated into two parts: (1) employee salary deferral contributions and (2) employer profit sharing contributions. If the employee is under 50 years of age, the 2017 contribution limit is $18,000. If the employee is 50 or older, an additional catch-up contribution of $6,000 is permitted for a total contribution limit of $24,000.

   Additionally, the employer can make profit-sharing contributions of 25 percent of the entity's income up to $36,000 for a maximum contribution of $54,000 if the plan owner is under 50 and $60,000 if the plan owner is 50 or older. The maximum compensation amount that can be used for calculating your contribution is $270,000 for 2017.

   The employee salary deferral can be up to 100 percent of your earned income for you and your spouse, up to the maximum annual contribution limits. This is on top of any Individual Retirement Account (IRA) contributions. The worksheet for determining the 401(k) calculation is found in IRS Publication 560.

2. The self-directed plan cannot only invest in standard assets like individual stocks, mutual funds, bonds, and money market certificates, but they can also invest in alternative assets such as real estate, private businesses, precious metals, loans and a host of other IRS permitted investments. There are no brokerage-imposed investment restrictions for self-directed plans.

3. The self-directed plan typically has a loan feature which permits the plan participant to borrow the lesser of $50,000 or 50 percent of the account balance, whichever is less. These funds can be used for any purpose but must be paid back to the plan over a five-year period at a reasonable interest rate. The rate most often stated is the prime rate plus one percent.

4. The self-directed plan typically provides the option to contribute after-tax dollars rather than before-tax dollars. This allows the plan holder to have a Roth sub-account, which means any earnings on the Roth portion of the account would be tax free. Usually, brokerage-directed accounts do not permit the Roth sub-account election.

5. The plan owner can establish a limited liability company or other entity and have the self-directed individual 401(k) plan purchase an ownership interest in the entity. This gives the plan owner, as fiduciary for the account, the flexibility to determine which investments are purchased by the entity and owned by the plan. It allows almost total control over the administration of the plan assets. Some term this check writing ability.

6. One of the absolute biggest benefits to having a self-directed individual 401(k) is that you can invest in leveraged, income-producing real estate investments. Leveraged (meaning borrowing money to purchase an investment) income-producing real estate investments are the best way to build assets in your retirement account that help you transition from relying on earned income to relying on passive income for your retirement needs. Mutual funds cannot be leveraged so they don't have the same ability to generate income at retirement. Mutual funds are liquidated during retirement while real estate is not. Real estate continues to appreciate in value during retirement while providing passive income to live on.

   Unlike self-directed IRAs, self-directed individual 401(k) plans are not subject to Unrelated Debt Financed Income (UDFI) tax. UDFI is a type of Unrelated Business Taxable Income (UBTI) which, if triggered, could subject an IRA account to a 35 percent tax on any income or gain attributable to the debt portion of an investment. Self-directed individual 401(k) plans are exempt from UDFI tax (IRC §514(c)(9).

7. When a person retires, the typical approach is to either leave the accumulated retirement earnings in the company's 401(k) plan, if permitted, or to take the money and put it in an IRA with a stock brokerage company, a bank or an insurance company. A better approach is to create a self-directed individual 401(k) account and transfer the money at retirement into that account. It provides all the same investment alternatives but gives maximum flexibility. A rollover or conversion can be done from any existing 401(k), 403(b), Money Purchase plans, Profit Sharing plans, Keogh plans, Define Benefit Pension plans, Traditional IRAs, SEP IRAs, or SIMPLE IRAs into a Self-directed Individual 401(k) with no tax consequences.

Eligibility Requirements for Setting up a Self-directed Individual 401(k)

To establish a self-directed individual 401(k) there are basically three general requirements:

1. The presence of self employment activity
2. Taxable compensation has been received during the year
3. The absence of full-time employees

One example of how an individual 401(k) plan would work would be a person who works for an employer but also does consulting on the side. The consulting income would be considered self-employment income thereby rendering the individual's business eligible for an individual 401(k) plan. The business can be a sole proprietorship, a partnership, a C-Corporation, an S-Corporation, or a limited liability company (LLC). With the exception of a spouse, the plan must not employ any full-time employees. A full-time employee is defined as one who works at least 1,000 hours per year for his/her employer. If you do not meet the eligibility requirements, consider establishing a SEP-IRA plan.

Permitted Self-Directed Retirement Account Investments

Numerous real estate related products and non-real estate products are permitted. Many accountants, financial planners, bankers and stockbrokers are not familiar with the wide array of investment choices that are available.

Permitted Self-Directed Retirement Account Investments	
Real Estate-Related Products	Non-Real Estate Products
Agricultural (Farm) Real Estate	Annuities
Build-to-Suit Real Estate Developments	Bonds
Commercial Real Estate	Commercial Paper
Construction Loans	Commodities
Fix-and-Flip Properties	Convertible Notes
Hard Money Loans	Equipment Leasing
Home Equity Loans	Factoring Accounts Payable
Home Mortgages/Take Out Loans	Franchises
International Real Estate	Hedge Funds
Discounted, Mezzanine & Bridge Loans	Mutual Funds
Participating Loans	Personal Property (see exceptions)
Privately-Traded Real Estate Investment Trusts	Privately-Held Companies
Publicly-Traded Real Estate Investment Trusts	Privately-Traded Stocks
Real Estate Leases	Publicly-Traded Stocks
Real Estate Options	Rights & Warrants
Residential Real Estate	Start Up Companies
Tax Deeds & Tax Liens	U.S Treasury Bills/Gold

Prohibited Investments in a Self-Directed Retirement Account

The IRS prohibits IRAs from acquiring several types of investments. They include the following:

Life Insurance

While annuities are permitted, whole life, universal life and variable universal life insurance policies are not permitted. Although the Incidental Benefit rule provides an exception for small amounts of coverage, this rule also applies to life insurance in qualified plans.

Certain Types of Derivative Trading

Derivatives include options and futures contracts on securities or commodities. Any type of trade or position that has unlimited or undefined risk, such as selling naked calls, is prohibited by the IRS. The reasoning behind this limitation is that the level of risk is inappropriate inside a retirement account that is designed to provide financial security during retirement.

Collectibles and Antiques

Furniture, wine or other alcoholic beverages, fine art, stamps, precious stones, porcelain and pottery, rugs, silver and dinnerware, jewelry, comic books, baseball cards, and other collectibles cannot be owned in the name of the IRA. That would also include priceless family heirlooms.

Your Personal Residence

You cannot hold any property that you personally use inside your IRA. This goes for both real and personal property. For instance, your primary residence, a second home, or a vacation home is prohibited. The Secretary of the Treasury has the right to define what type of tangible personal property may and may not be held in an IRA.

Certain Types of Coins

In general, you cannot hold any type of coin made from gold, platinum, or other precious metal inside an IRA. The IRS does have a list of exceptions, including:

- American Eagle coins that have never been circulated,
- Proofs of American Eagle coins,
- American buffalo coins,
- Canadian Maple Leaf coins, and
- Australian Gold Philharmonic coins.

To be allowed in an IRA, the coin's actual currency value must exceed its value as a collector's item.

Prohibited Transaction Rule Basics

A prohibited transaction is any improper transaction between an IRA and a disqualified person, as defined in IRS Publication 590. Disqualified persons include the IRA owner and certain family members. For example, since your IRA is restricted from buying or selling investments that you personally own, a prohibited transaction would occur if you use your IRA to buy real estate that you already own in your personal name.

Prohibited Transactions

Most retirement plan investors have never heard of prohibited transaction rules because they invest primarily in publicly-traded mutual funds and stocks. These rules are important when you have a self-directed retirement account because you are now in charge of the types of investments that are purchased by that account and with whom you intend to transact with.

Prohibited transaction rules do not specify what your IRA may invest in, but rather they restrict who your IRA may transact with. The question becomes, who is on the other side of the transaction with your IRA?

The consequence of a prohibited transaction between an IRA and the IRA owner can be very serious. It can disqualify the entire IRA and result in a distribution of the total amount in the IRA to the IRA owner personally. The distribution will be subject to all applicable taxes and penalties upon withdrawal. Prohibited transaction rules are the same for Roth IRAs as they are for Traditional IRAs.

There are two different categories of prohibited transactions under the rules: per se prohibited transactions and self-dealing prohibited transactions.

Who is a Disqualified Person to my IRA?

A disqualified person to your IRA includes the IRA owner and the lineal ascendants and descendants of the IRA owner, such as: the IRA owner, the IRA owner's spouse, parents, grandparents, children, spouses of children. Also included as disqualified persons are companies in which the IRA owner or other disqualified person has more than 50% control. Why are these individuals and entities considered disqualified persons?

The self-directed IRA account owner is a disqualified person because he or she is a fiduciary to the IRA and makes the investment decisions on behalf of the IRA and, as such, has the ability to enter into a transaction with the intent to avoid or unfairly minimize taxes IRC §4975 (e)(2)(A). Certain close famiy members of the IRA owner are disqualified for the same reason.

A corporation, partnership, LLC,, trust or estate which is owned 50 percent or more by disqualified persons could also wield undue influence over the IRA. The 50 percent controlling interest includes:

- 50 percent or more of the voting authority of all classes of stock, or
- 50 percent or more of the capital interests or profits of the entity, or
- 50 percent or more of the beneficial interest of a trust or unincorporated business. IRC §4975 (e)(2)(G).

For example, if an IRA owner and his spouse owned 60 percent of an LLC, then that LLC would be a disqualified person as to the IRA. If the IRA owner and all other disqualified persons own 49 percent or less of the company and other unrelated third parties own the other 51 percent of the company, then the company is not disqualified person to the IRA. A company's officers, directors, and 10 percent or more shareholders are only disqualified to an IRA when the IRA owner or other disqualified family member owns 50 percent or more of the company.

Not all family members are disqualified persons. Brothers, sisters, cousins, aunts, uncles, nieces and nephews are not disqualified persons nor are friends, co-workers neighbors or other third parties. The following diagrams will help you determine whether or not a per se prohibited transaction has occurred.

Diagram of Self-Dealing Relationships

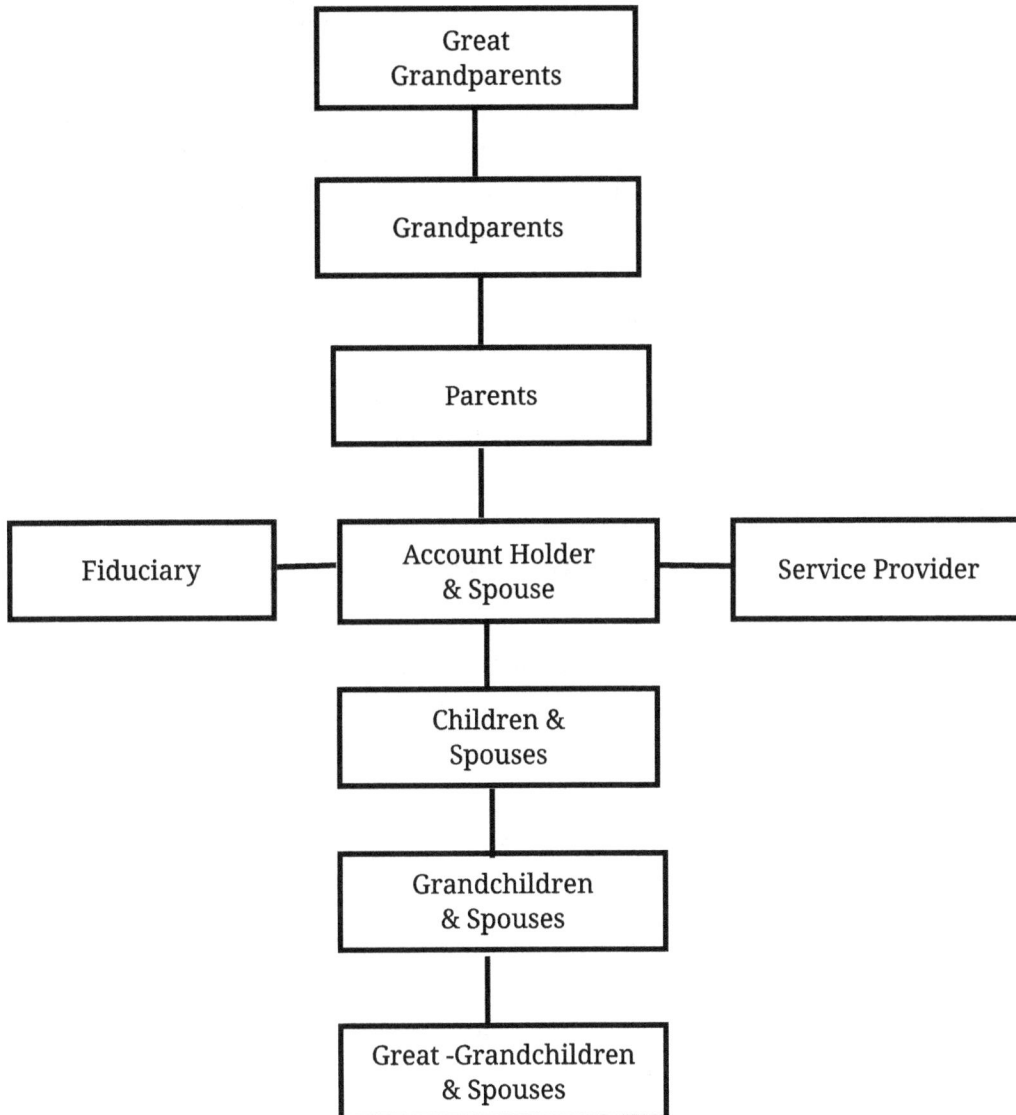

```
                    ┌──────────────────┐
                    │      Great       │
                    │   Grandparents   │
                    └──────────────────┘
                             │
                    ┌──────────────────┐
                    │   Grandparents   │
                    └──────────────────┘
                             │
                    ┌──────────────────┐
                    │     Parents      │
                    └──────────────────┘
                             │
  ┌────────────┐    ┌──────────────────┐    ┌──────────────────┐
  │  Fiduciary │────│  Account Holder  │────│ Service Provider │
  └────────────┘    │     & Spouse     │    └──────────────────┘
                    └──────────────────┘
                             │
                    ┌──────────────────┐
                    │    Children &    │
                    │     Spouses      │
                    └──────────────────┘
                             │
                    ┌──────────────────┐
                    │  Grandchildren   │
                    │    & Spouses     │
                    └──────────────────┘
                             │
                    ┌──────────────────┐
                    │ Great-Grandchildren │
                    │     & Spouses    │
                    └──────────────────┘
```

What Companies are Prohibited to my IRA?

The rationale behind the 50 percent controlling interest provision is that if non-disqualified owners are in majority control of the company, they would only decide to sell at a legitimate purchase price and would not allow shares to be sold below its fair market value to the IRA.

Suppose there is an LLC with ownership interests owned 33 percent by you, 33 percent by your brother, and 33 percent owned by your aunt and it owns rental property. Can your IRA buy the property from the LLC? The answer is yes, because you own less than 50 percent and the other two owners are not disqualified persons. IRC §4975 (e)(2)(G).

Now suppose that you want to sell your 33 percent ownership in the LLC mentioned above to your self-directed Roth IRA, can yo do this? The answer is no, because the shares you are selling are owned by you personally and you are a disqualified person to your IRA, since you are the owner. If your Roth IRA is investing in the company, it must purchase its shares from the other two owners, i.e., the brother or the aunt, who are not disqualified persons.

Self-Dealing Prohibited Transactions

Self-dealing is the second type of prohibited transaction. Self-dealing occurs when an IRA owner or other disqualified person benefits personally from the IRA's investments rather than the IRA benefiting from its investments. IRC §4975 (c)(1)(D), (E), and (F). A self-dealing prohibited transaction is also referred to as a conflict of interest prohibited transaction.

The IRS, in IRC §4975 (c)(1), has stated that an IRA is engaged in self-dealing prohibited transactions when a direct or indirect:

(d) transfer to, or use by or for the benefit of, a disqualified person of the income or assets of a plan; or

(e) act by a disqualified person who is a fiduciary whereby he deals with the income or assets of a plan in his own interest or for his own account, or

(f) receipt of any consideration for his own personal account by any disqualified person who is a fiduciary from any party dealing with the plan in connection with a transaction involving the income or assets of the plan.

Paragraph (D) applies to all disqualified persons while paragraphs (E) and (F) apply only to the IRA owner, who is the fiduciary of the IRA. Self-dealing prohibited transactions are based on subjective factors that can be difficult to determine, but they are best analyzed under the language of paragraph (D), which gives the broadest interpretation.

"For example, let's say you're a real estate agent, and you act as the agent and purchase an investment property with your self-directed IRA. As part of the purchase, you receive the buyer's agent commission. Since you were the buyer's agent on the transaction, this commission, unfortunately, constitutes a self dealing prohibited transaction because the IRA owner personally benefited from the IRA's transaction by receiving the commission. As a result, if you are serving as the real estate agent for your own IRA, then you would need to waive your commission or would need to hire a non-disqualified person to serve as the agent for the self directed IRA's purchase of the investment property.

"There is an argument that a broker commission may be 'reasonable compensation' under IRC §4975 (d)(10), and exempt from the prohibited transaction rules. However, the reasonable compensation exemption for real estate commissions received by a disqualified person, has not been tested in Court nor has it been specifically endorsed by the IRS or DOL. As a result, IRA owners should not rely on it and should avoid commissions or compensation to disqualified persons.

"Another common example is a rental property owned by your IRA. While you may lease the property to non-disqualified persons, you may not personally stay at or use the property Use of property violates the self dealing rules as you end up personally benefiting from your retirement account's investments by getting a free stay. If you paid rent at the same rate that other tenants paid, then you wouldn't be personally benefiting and wouldn't have a self dealing prohibited transaction. Instead, you would have a per se prohibited transaction because the rent payment would be a payment to the IRA from a disqualified person. Therefore, using the assets of your retirement account for personal use (or use by another disqualified person) will create a prohibited transaction whether you pay for them (per se prohibited transaction) or whether you receive them for free (self dealing prohibited transaction)."[1]

The Consequences of a Prohibited Transaction

The consequences of a prohibited transaction differ, depending on whether the disqualified person is the IRA owner or another party. The most common type of prohibited transaction is between an IRA owner and his/her IRA.

---

[1] Mat Sorensen, *The Self Directed IRA Handbook*, SoKoh Publishing, LLC, 2014, 56-57.

If an IRA owner engages in a prohibited transaction with his, or her, own IRA, the entire IRA is disqualified. Disqualification results in distribution of the entire account, based on the fair market value of all assets in the account as of January 1 of the year in which the prohibited transaction occurred. IRC §4975 (c)(3), IRC §408 (e)(2)(A). Distribution of an IRA resulted in possible taxes on the amount distributed, early withdrawal penalties, if the person is under 59 1/2 years of age, and revocation of the favorable tax treatment for IRA investments that occurred after the prohibited transaction.

Review Questions

1. A Self-Directed retirement account does not allow the account owner to invest in other types of investments.

   A. True
   B. False

2. Which of the following retirement accounts can be self-directed?

   A. Individual Retirement Account (IRA)
   B. 401(k)
   C. SEP-IRA
   D. All of the above

3. Most banks, stock brokerages, insurance companies, and financial planners affiliated with independent broker-dealers, will not permit the IRAs they manage to be self-directed.

   A. True
   B. False

4. Which of the following is NOT a benefit of a Self-Directed 401(k) plan?

   A. A Self-Directed plan can invest in both traditional and alternative investments.
   B. A Self-Directed plan stipulates that you must contribute less than the standard plan.
   C. A Self-Directed plan has a loan feature which permits plan participants to borrow $50,000 or 50 percent of the account balance, whichever is less.
   D. A Self-Directed plan typically provides the option to contribute after-tax dollars rather than before-tax dollars.

5. Which of the following is a benefit of a Self-Directed 401(k) plan?

   A. The plan owner can establish and purchase an ownership interest in a limited liability company.
   B. The plan owner can invest in leveraged, income-producing real estate investments with some restrictions.
   C. The Self-Directed 401(k) is not subject to Unrelated Debt Financed Income Tax.
   D. All of the above

6. Self-Directed retirement accounts can invest in not only all the traditional permitted investments but also a number of real estate related investment products.

   A. True
   B. False

7. Which of the following are permitted investments in a Self-Directed retirement account?

   A. Life Insurance
   B. Collectibles and antiques
   C. Real estate related products
   D. Your personal residence

8. Which of the following is NOT a permitted investment in a Self-Directed retirement account?

   A. Life Insurance
   B. Collectibles and antiques
   C. Your personal residence
   D. All of the above

9. Of the following, who would NOT be considered a disqualified person to a Self-Directed IRA?

   A. A brother, sister, cousin, aunt, uncle, niece, nephew or friend of the account holder
   B. The account holder and his/her spouse
   C. The parents and grandparents of the account holder
   D. The children and grandchildren of the account holder and their spouses

10. Self-dealing occurs when an IRA owner or other disqualified person benefits personally from the IRA's investments rather than the IRA benefiting from its investments. Based on this definition, which of the following transactions would be considered self-dealing?

    A. The account owner buys an interest in a company they already control
    B. The account owner lends money from his account to a disqualified person
    C. The account owner uses an investment property purchased by the IRA for his/her personal residence
    D. All of the above

11. If an IRA owner engages in a prohibited transaction, which of the following may occur?

    A. The IRA may be deemed disqualified.
    B. The disqualification will result in the entire account being deemed distributed.
    C. Early withdrawal penalties and the payment of taxes on the entire account may result.
    D. All of the above

12. Which of the following investments are NOT permitted in a Self-Directed retirement account?

    A. Life insurance
    B. Commercial real estate
    C. Publicly-traded stocks
    D. Tax deeds & tax liens

Section Five
Administrators & Custodians

Objectives

- **To define Third Party Administrators (TPA) and custodians**
- **To explain how to set up a self-directed retirement account**
- **To discuss rollovers, conversions, and Roth conversions**

Administrators & Custodians

Although the plan owner could act as his/her own Trustee, it is prudent to work with a Third Party Administrator (TPA) who is familiar with the technical reporting requirements of the IRS. When you place your money in an account with them, they are required by law to hold your money in an account with a Custodian. A Custodian is generally a federally insured bank or credit union.

The TPA and the Custodian can be the same, but chances are, in a self-directed situation, the TPA is not the Custodian. The terms Administrator and Custodian are frequently used interchangeably, so it becomes a bit confusing. Just remember that a Custodian is always the financial institution that holds your money, regardless of who handles the administration of your account. In addition to knowing who the Administrator is, always find out who the custodian is.

A TPA is an individual (organization) who sets up, manages, and otherwise administers retirement accounts. A TPA should be hired to set up a self-directed retirement account. The primary role of a TPA is to set up a retirement account to ensure the plan meets IRS regulations so it gets the allowable deductions. Several types of TPAs are available. A retirement account should not be managed without a TPA; otherwise, the owner of the account will be personally responsible for meeting all the IRS regulations. Appointing a TPA will cost a small fee when an account is opened, plus additional transactions fees and administrative costs as a person invests.

Beyond cost, the TPA will limit the owner's control of the account. Changes to the account are handled through direction letters. Most TPAs are not financial institutions, so they affiliate with a bank or other financial institution to handle the custodial responsibilities of safeguarding the money in a retirement account.

A self-directed retirement account should be held with a custodian that allows investments into real estate and other non-traditional investments. All custodians have a relationship with a primary bank that handles client deposits. Custodians charge annual fees or transaction fees or combination of the two. Each custodian is required to provide prospective clients with a fee schedule and a disclosure statement. These items can usually be obtained on the company's website.

If the custodian is a bank, your money will be insured by the Federal Deposit Insurance Corporation (FDIC), which is an independent agency of the United States government. The FDIC protects depositors of insured banks located in the United States against the loss of the deposits of an insured bank for a sum of up to $250,000 per depositor, per insured bank, for each account ownership category. There are nationally-chartered and state-chartered banks. All national banks and most state banks have FDIC insurance, but there are a handful of state banks that do not have FDIC insurance.

If the custodian is a credit union rather than a bank, it will be insured by the National Credit Union Share Insurance Fund (NCUSIF) for an amount up to $250,000 on any single ownership account. All federally-insured credit unions are members of the National Credit Union Administration (NCUA). Both federally-insured banks and federally-insured credit unions are backed by the full faith and credit of the United States up to $250,000 per single account. There are federally-chartered and state-chartered credit unions. Some state-chartered credit unions are insured by private insurers and are not backed by the full faith and credit of the United States government. Whether your custodian is a bank or credit union, be careful with whom you do business.

If you have more than $250,000 in your IRA or 401(k), you better make sure that the custodian your administrator is using is a financial institution that will not go broke. If they do, you stand to lose everything above $250,000. Make sure your Administrator has made adequate arrangements to insure that you never lose the money you have in your retirement account.

A custodian is an IRS-approved financial institution such as a bank or a brokerage company that is entrusted with the responsibility of safeguarding the assets of a client's retirement account. Individuals may not act as custodians. Non-financial institutions must obtain specific approval from the IRS to act as a custodian.

Characteristics of a Good TPA
IRS approved
Title authority to handle real estate transactions
Financially sound
Experienced
Knowledgeable
Service-oriented

Find a Qualified Third Party Administrator/Custodian

Several national companies and some regional companies are good administrators. The three largest TPAs are The Entrust Group (www.theentrustgroup.com), Equity Trust Company (www.trust-etc.com), and Pensco Trust Company (www.pensco.com). In addition, there are several smaller TPAs, one of which is Mountain West IRA (www.mwira.com).

How to Set Up a Self-directed Individual 401(k) Account

Each TPA/Custodian that handles self-directed individual 401(k) accounts has a packet of information that they will email to you. Setting up an individual 401(k) account is more complicated than establishing an IRA. The typical plan documents include the following:

- Adoption Agreement
- Basic Plan Document
- Plan Description
- Appointment of Trustee(s)
- Action of Board of Directors
- Beneficiary Designation
- Deferral Agreement
- Loan Procedures and Loan Documentation
- Transfer Request and/or Letter of Acceptance
- Election not to participate
- Newly assigned EIN (Employer Identification Number) for the plan
- IRS Determination Letter - stating the Plan meets the requirements of a Qualified Plan

While this is truly a lot of paperwork to complete, it only has to be done once. After the plan is in place, it operates just like any other retirement account.

See Appendices A, B and C.

A self-directed individual 401(k) isn't for everyone, but if you and your spouse have no full-time employees and you are a sole practitioner, self-employed consultant, real estate professional, sales person, private contractor or any one of a myriad of other "1099" independent contractors, you are a perfect candidate for a self-directed individual 401(k) plan. If you are retiring from your employer and elect to move your retirement savings to an account that you control, a self-directed individual 401(k) account is better than an IRA.

A self-directed individual 401(k) account works well for anyone who wants to invest directly in real estate because 401(k)s are not subject to Unrelated Debt Financed Income (UDFI) tax. There are very good Third Party Administrators/Custodians out there who can help you establish an account and do the administration for a fee. It does take some effort to fill out the paperwork and meet the qualifications, but it is well worth the time and effort.

Rollovers and Conversions

A rollover is a transfer of funds from one retirement account to another. It occurs either through a direct transfer of the assets held or by liquidation of the assets and the custodian holding the account transferring the cash to a self-directed retirement account custodian. In general, anyone with a Traditional IRA or 401(k) may roll over their account to another self-directed Traditional IRA or 401(k). A company 401(k) could be rolled over to a Solo or Individual 401(k). Usually, people are permitted only one rollover per year from each IRA owned. If a Traditional IRA or 401(k) was rolled into a Roth IRA or 401(k), there would be recognition of income and the required taxes would need to be paid.

A conversion is the process of taking a tax-deferred retirement account and converting it to a tax-free retirement account. Essentially, a Traditional IRA or 401(k) is converted into a Roth IRA or Roth 401(k). When a conversion is made, the IRS requires that all converted funds be considered earnings in the year of the conversion and taxed at ordinary income tax rates.

See Appendix D: Transfer & Rollover Forms

Important Additional Considerations

Roth Conversions

The best way to minimize Required Minimum Distributions (RMDs) is to take the money out of a Traditional IRA prior to age 70. Of course, when one does this, they lose the benefit of tax-free growth unless they immediately roll the money into a Roth IRA. Many fully or partially retired investors opt to convert part of their Traditional IRA to a Roth IRA to lower their future RMDs.

Review Questions

1. When dealing with Self-Directed retirement accounts, it is prudent to work with a Third Party Administrator (TPA) who is familiar with the technical reporting requirements of the IRS.

    A. True
    B. False

2. A Third Party Administrator (TPA) is always a custodian.

    A. True
    B. False

3. The primary role of a Third Party Administrator would be:

    A. To hold the money for the retirement plan
    B. To pay for the costs of administration of the retirement plan
    C. To set up the retirement account to ensure the plan meets IRS regulations
    D. To choose the investments for the retirement account

4. Which of the following would be considered a Custodian of a Self-Directed retirement plan?

    A. A federally-insured bank
    B. A federally-insured credit union
    C. Both A and B
    D. Neither A nor B

5. Which of the following would be considered a duty of a Third Party Administrator?

    A. To set up the self-directed retirement account
    B. To ensure the self-directed retirement account meets IRS regulations
    C. To report the activity of the self-directed retirement account to the IRS
    D. All of the above

6. In setting up a Self-Directed 401(k) plan, the typical plan documents would include:

    A. An Adoption Agreement
    B. A Basic Plan Document
    C. The Appointment of a Trustee
    D. All of the above

7. A Self-Directed individual 401(k) would be appropriate for which of the following?

    A. A self-employed consultant
    B. A real estate professional
    C. Both A and B above
    D. Neither A nor B above

8. A transfer of funds from one retirement account to another is called:

    A. A conversion
    B. A rollover
    C. A rollunder
    D. A mistake

9. The process of taking a tax-deferred retirement account and changing it to a tax-free retirement account is called:

    A. A rollover
    B. A rollunder
    C. A conversion
    D. A mistake

Section Six
Buying Real Estate with a Self-Directed Retirement Account

Objectives

- **To discuss buying real estate with a self-directed retirement account**
- **To explain permissible and prohibited management actions by disqualified persons**
- **To introduce a checklist for IRA owners of real estate**

Buying Real Estate with a Self-Directed Retirement Account[1]

Real estate is the most common investment made by self-directed retirement plan investors. Self-directed IRAs and 401(k)s may invest in all types of real estate, including residential (both single family and multifamily units) and commercial properties, new construction and development, land, water, or mineral rights.

Several points should be considered when buying real estate with a self-directed retirement account. When considering the list of key points stated below, please keep in mind that the same key points apply when purchasing real estate with a self-directed 401(k) as when purchasing a property with a self-directed IRA.[2] The key points are as follows:

- Real estate owned by a retirement plan must always be held for investment, and the IRA owner and disqualified persons (e.g., certain family) cannot live in or benefit from the property

- All income derived from the property should be paid directly to the IRA custodian for the benefit of the IRA, and all expenses from the property should be paid from the IRA (except when an IRA/LLC is used)

---

[1]Mat Sorensen, *The Self Directed IRA Handbook* (SoKoh Publishing, LLC, 2014), 110-123. Note: With the author's permission, this entire section came almost verbatim from Chapter 9: Self Directed IRAs and Real Estate. In some instances, I have taken the liberty to shorten sentences for brevity, being careful not to alter the author's meaning or context.

[2]See Appendix E: Direction of Investment – Private Placement

- When purchasing real estate with an IRA, the IRA must be listed on the contract as the buyer, and it is the custodian of the IRA and not the IRA owner who signs the contract to bind the IRA. For example, the buyer to the contract would be ABC Trust Company FBO Sally Jones IRA. Once the contract is ready to be signed, the IRA owner will send it to his or her self directed IRA custodian with a direction of investment form, instructing the custodian to sign the contract for the IRA. In most instances, the custodian of the IRA will require the IRA owner to sign the contract as read and approved so the custodian is certain that the IRA owner has read the terms and approved them for his or her IRA.

- Remember, the IRA is buying the property and not the IRA owner, so all contracts must be signed by the IRA custodian, who is the only party that can legally bind the IRA.

- All funds due by the buyer and relating to the purchase of the property must be paid by the IRA, including: earnest money deposit or down payment, closing costs, inspection and due diligence costs, and the final funds necessary to close the property.

- Since the IRA owner is a disqualified person to his or her own IRA, the IRA owner (and any other disqualified person) cannot make the earnest money deposit and cannot cover other expenses to the property with personal funds outside of the IRA.

- The purchase contract for a property cannot be assigned from a disqualified person (e.g., IRA owner) to an IRA. Similarly, the IRA cannot assign a property to the IRA owner or other disqualified persons.

- Assignment of a contract between an IRA and a disqualified person is a per se prohibited transaction.[2] So, for example, it is not acceptable to get a property under contract in your personal name or under a company you own and then later assign it to your IRA.

- A real estate contract could be assigned to the IRA from someone else who is not a disqualified person; conversely, any assignment from a disqualified person will likely constitute a prohibited transaction.

---

[2] See Section on Prohibited Transactions

- In the event that an IRA owner mistakenly enters into a contract in their person name, then the IRA owner should seek to unwind the contract in his or her person name with the seller and should obtain a new contract, properly listing the IRA as the buyer.

- Any earnest money deposit made personally should be returned and the IRA should then pay the earnest money deposit and bear those expenses and contract requirements in the new contract.

- If the contract cannot be undone in the IRA owner's personal name, then an addendum to the contract can be added, clarifying that the buyer is the IRA. The addendum should not transfer or assign the contract but shall instead clarify who the buyer is. For example, if John Smith is intending to use his IRA to buy a property and mistakenly listed himself as the buyer, then an addendum to the contract can be added, clarifying that the buyer is not John Smith but is ABC Trust Company FBO John Smith IRA. This should be done only as a second resort and in the case of mistake as there are some prohibited transaction issues involved when doing an addendum such as this. Again, the first attempt to correct the contract should always be unwinding the contract in the IRA owner's name and obtaining a new contract with the IRA correctly listed as the buyer. The addendum practice should only be used in the case of mistake and when completing a new contract if the IRA's name is not possible.

- An IRA can obtain a loan to purchase real estate, however, the loan must not result in an extension of credit prohibited transaction under IRC §4975 (c)(1)(B). An extension of credit prohibited transaction will occur when an IRA owner's credit qualifies the IRA for the loan or when the IRA owner (or other disqualified person) personally guarantees a loan for the IRA. As a result, any loan obtained by the IRA to purchase real estate must be a non-recourse loan. A non-recourse loan is a loan where the lender's sole recourse in the event of default is to foreclose and take the property back. The lender does not have any additional recourse against the IRA or the IRA owner. Additionally, the qualification rules and criteria for an IRA compliant non-recourse loan are solely based on the property being used to secure the loan.

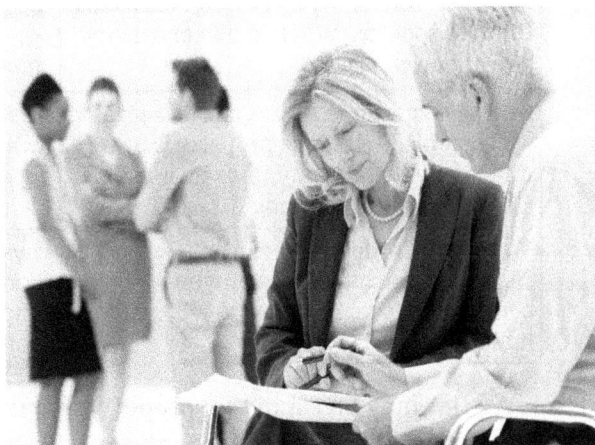

- If the IRA is going to be on title to real property with other owners, then the multiple-party form of ownership must be tenants in common. Other forms of multiple-party title ownership, such as joint tenancy and tenants by the entirety, should not be used because those ownership interests have characteristics whereby ownership passes to the other party on title following the death of the owner.

- When an IRA-owned property is held for rent, it must be structured such that rental income is received by the IRA, and expenses are paid by the IRA. The IRA owner and other disqualified persons cannot personally be the "middle man" by paying expenses personally or by collecting the rent in their personal account and ten forwarding the funds to the IRA.

- When managing IRA investment assets, the IRA owner should limit his or her activities to administrative and investment oversight tasks. While it is permissible to administer the investment, it is generally viewed as impermissible to physically work on investment assets (such as rental real estate) since such actions can constitute a per se prohibited or self-dealing prohibited transaction. IRC §4975(c)(1)(C). The following table outlines what activities are permissible and what activities are prohibited.

| Permissible and Prohibited Management Actions by Disqualified Persons ||
Permissible	Prohibited
Making decisions as to the property manager or tenants. Making all decisions for the property. When to buy or sell and at what price, etc.	Taking title or entering into contracts in the IRA owner's personal name as opposed to the IRA (the IRA custodian should sign all contracts).
Setting terms for the lease or other legal agreements. When the property is owned directly by the IRA, any contract must be signed by the IRA custodian.	Receiving rental income in the IRA owner's personal account or paying IRA expenses from a personal account of the IRA owner.
Visiting the property and overseeing repairs and maintenance. Hiring contractors to do repairs and maintenance.	Physically working on the property. Work by the IRA owner or other disqualified person(s) on the property is prohibited.

- An IRA may invest in real property that is being developed and may also purchase properties on a short-term basis and flip them for profit. A retirement plan's investment in real estate development or on real estate flips, however, can subject the IRA to a tax known as Unrelated Business Income Tax (UBIT tax). IRC §511, 512. The UBIT tax applies to the net profits that arise from the development of real property or from property held without any investment intent (e.g., bought and held immediately for sale). Real property held for investment (e.g., rental, or held for one year or more) is exempt from UBIT tax so all efforts should be made to hold the property for investment rather than hold the property for development and immediate sale. Additionally, if a property is acquired with debt financing the IRA may also be subject to unrelated debt-financed income tax (UDFI). Please note that IRAs are subject to UBIT and UDFI but 401(k)s are not.

- **A note of caution:** The IRA owner should avoid overextending the IRA where it may be unable to cover unexpected property expenses. If IRA funds are inadequate to cover property expenses, it is left in a difficult position. The IRA owner cannot just personally pay the expenses owed by the IRA. Paying the expenses personally would constitute a prohibited transaction. As a rule of thumb, the IRA should maintain 10% of the purchase price in cash to cover unexpected expenses.

Checklist for IRA Ownership of Real Estate

▸ Is the contract and deed/title in the IRA's name?

▸ Did the IRA custodian sign the contract and legal agreements for the IRA, or where applicable, did the manager of the IRA/LLC sign them?

▸ Did the IRA owner refrain from using personal expenses in purchasing and maintaining the property?

▸ If the IRA obtained a loan to purchase the property, was the loan nonrecourse?

▸ Is the IRA owner aware of possible UDFI taxes on any net profits from the debt?

▸ Is the IRA custodian, the property manager, or a property established IRA/LLC, receiving the rental income and paying the expenses for the property?

▸ Does the IRA have sufficient capital available to over an unexpected property expense?

▸ Is the IRA owner holding the property for investment?

▸ Is the IRA owner or other disqualified persons avoiding personal use or benefit from the property?

▸ When applicable, was the broker or agent in the transaction a no-disqualified person?

▸ Did the IRA owner refrain from personally benefiting from the IRA's purchase?

Special Considerations When Buying Real Estate

Real estate is typically a great investment for a self-directed retirement account. Some issues should be addressed when purchasing real estate. The first consideration is whether the real estate is purchased with all cash or with some cash and some debt financing. An all-cash purchase is considered an unleveraged investment. A debt-financed purchase is considered a leveraged investment. One of the benefits of purchasing real estate with debt financing is the possibility of achieving higher returns using leverage.

Leveraged and Unleveraged Investments

A leveraged real estate investment is one that uses both investor capital and borrowed funds to acquire the property. An unleveraged investment is an investment that does not have any debt associated with the property.

Typically, a self-directed retirement account cannot borrow money to finance part of the purchase of the property unless the financing is non-recourse, which means that the self- directed retirement account, or its owner or spouse, is not required to personally guarantee the loan. Should a default occur on the loan, the lender looks solely to the real estate asset for repayment and has no recourse against the self-directed retirement account investor for the repayment of the loan.

It is permissible for a builder, developer or some other guarantor to personally guarantee the debt on the project and then raise equity capital through self-directed retirement account investors. This type of investment meets the requirement of having the real estate asset non- recourse to the self-directed retirement account investor, but takes advantage of having debt financing as part of the acquisition cost. The financing may not be personally guaranteed by a disqualified person.

If a self-directed IRA acquires a business and uses nonrecourse debt in the acquisition, a portion of the income and gain on sale is subject to Unrelated Business Income Tax (UBIT). Unrelated Business Income exists when a tax-exempt entity engages in a business purpose that is unrelated to its tax-exempt purpose.

If an IRA uses debt financing to acquire real estate, it is subject to the payment of a tax on that portion of the income attributable to the debt financing. The income derived from the debt financed portion is called Unrelated Debt Financed Income (UDFI). UDFI is a subset of the IRS code section described as unrelated business taxable income.

Investment income that would otherwise be excluded from an exempt organization's unrelated business taxable income must be included to the extent it is derived from debt- financed property. The amount of income included is proportionate to the debt on the property. In general, the term "debt-financed property" means any property held to produce income (including gain from its disposition) for which there is an acquisition indebtedness at any time during the tax year (or during the 12-month period before the date of the property's disposal, if it was disposed of during the tax year). However, acquisition indebtedness does not include debt incurred by a qualified organization in acquiring or improving any real property. *(IRS Publication 598)*

Is a person subject to Unrelated Business Taxable Income (UBTI) tax on unrelated debt-financed income in a Solo 401(k) plan? The answer is no.

Unlike a self-directed IRA, LLC, when a Solo 401(k) plan uses nonrecourse leverage to purchase real estate that is leveraged, it is exempt from paying any UBTI tax on the income or gain generated. When an IRA buys real estate that is leveraged with mortgage financing, it creates unrelated debt-financed income (a type of unrelated business taxable income) on which taxes must be paid. A Solo 401(k) plan is exempt from UDFI pursuant to Internal Revenue Code Section 514(c)(9).

> "With the UBTI tax rates at approximately 35% (the Trust Rate), the Solo 401(k) plan offers real estate investors looking to use nonrecourse leverage in a transaction with a tax efficient solution." *(IRA Financial Group)*

Why does this exemption apply to 401(k) plans and not IRAs?

> "When Internal Revenue Code Section 514(c)(9) was enacted in1980, it applied only to qualified pension, profit sharing, and stock bonus plans, but its scope was broadened in1984 to include schools, colleges, and universities. The provision brings the history of Internal Revenue Code Section 514 full circle by exempting some organizations, such as 401(k) Qualified Plan[s], from tax on income from the very sort of leveraged real estate deals that provoked the enactment of the predecessor of Internal Revenue Code Section 514 in 1950, As per the legislative history, the only reason given in the committee reports for the exemption is that some people wanted it 'Trustees of these plans are desirous of investing in real estate for diversification and to offset inflation, Debt-financing is common in real estate investments." *(IRA Financial Group)*

Some may question whether real estate can generate higher returns through a self-directed IRA, since the debt-financed portion of the income is taxed. However, almost any real estate investment that is good for a private investor is an even better investment when purchased through a self-directed retirement account.

UBTI, UBIT, and UDFI

Unrelated Business Taxable Income

Two types of UBTl exist: 1) Income arising from the conduct of an unrelated trade or business that is regularly carried on; and 2) Debt-financed income, which is usually income in the form of rent, interest or royalties arising from financed property. A trade or business is any activity carried on to produce income from the sale of goods or the performance of services in the same manner as a for-profit business.

Deductions, both direct and indirect, which are proximate and primary to the generation of the taxable income, can be used to offset UBTI. These would include salaries, interest payments, maintenance expenses, and depreciation. UBTI can be mitigated, to some extent, by depreciating the assets using cost segregation, which segregates the cost of each construction component and depreciates it over its useful life. Although it is a straight line method for computing depreciation, it tends to load more depreciation in the early years because many components are written off over a shorter useful life.

If a self-directed retirement account purchases a trade or business that is unrelated to its primary purpose, then the income earned is subject to a tax on that income.(Congress offered tax-deferred retirement accounts primarily to encourage retirement savings to augment social security benefits).

Unrelated Business Income Tax

UBIT is a tax imposed on the unrelated business income generated by a tax exempt entity, of which a self-directed retirement account is one. UBIT is calculated by using the tax rates for estates and trusts. The current trust rates are as follows:

- If taxable income is less than $2,200, the base tax is zero plus 15 percent over zero
- If taxable income is between $2,200 and $5,150, the base tax is $330 plus 25 percent over $2,200
- If taxable income is between $5,150 and $7,850, the base tax is $1,067.50 plus 28 percent over $5,150
- If taxable income is between $7,850 and $10,700, the base tax is $1,823.50 plus 33 percent over $7,850
- If taxable income is between $10,700 or more, the base tax is $2,764 plus 35 percent over $10,700

UBTI is a complicated area of the Internal Revenue Code and is best determined by a professional accountant or qualified tax adviser to avoid any unintended consequences.

Unrelated Debt Financed Income

UDFI is income generated by an IRA, or other retirement plan, through the use of debt financing or leverage. UDFI is taxed much like UBTI and is similarly as complicated. UDFI only applies to the profit realized through debt and is based on the highest amount of leverage carried within the past 12 months. Refer to IRC§ 514(a)(1).

UDFI does not apply if the debt is paid off 12 months prior to the sale of the property. If the loan for a self-directed IRA can be paid off early, UBIT may not have to be paid.

It should be noted that even with the constraint of UBTI and UDFI, it is likely that the return for a self-directed retirement account is likely to be greater using leverage and

67

debt financing than purchasing an asset on an unleveraged, debt-free basis. Consult an accountant, tax advisor and investment advisor to determine the effects of UBT! and UDFI on a return prior to investing in an asset that has debt financing as an element of the capital structure.

Depreciation & Gain on Sale

With regard to real estate, depreciation is an allowance made for the loss in value due to age and wear of a property. In accounting, an expense is recorded each year to allocate a portion of the cost associated with the diminished useful life of the asset. The expense can be deducted from income as part of the determination of net income. Therefore, the more depreciation write-off in any given year, the less the tax that has to be paid on the net income.

With regard to self-directed IRAs, if there is no debt financing on the property, depreciation would not be applicable nor would there be any recognition of gain on the sale of the asset. In a traditional IRA, the recognition of income is deferred until withdrawals begin, at which time, all income is taxed at ordinary income tax rates.In a Roth IRA, all withdrawals are tax- free, so there is never any recognition of income.With regard to a self-directed traditional or Roth 401(k), the same principles apply.

However, when debt financing is associated with a self-directed IRA, the application of depreciation would be applicable to that portion of the income that is attributable to the debt financing. Likewise, it would also relate to any depreciation recapture for the portion of the income attributable to the debt financing on the recognition of gain at the time of sale. When debt financing is associated with a self-directed 401(k), depreciation and capital gain recognition are not relevant because UDFI rules do not apply. This is an area of the law that is best left to the experts. Consult an accountant or tax adviser when dealing with these situations.

When applying depreciation, self-directed retirement accounts are only permitted to use straight line depreciation. The straight line method of depreciation expenses a portion of the original cost in equal increments over the useful life of the asset.

Residential income property must be depreciated over a 27.5 year period. Commercial income property must be depreciated over 39 years. Use cost segregation to achieve a higher straight line depreciation allocation in the first years of the investment. Cost segregation maximizes the tax savings by adjusting the timing of the deductions for tax purposes. Cost segregation identifies the various components comprising the real estate and allocates a useful life and value for each component.

Cost segregation identifies building costs that would typically be depreciated over a 27.5- or 39- year period and reclassifies them to permit a shorter depreciation period. Costs for non- structural elements, such as wall coverings, carpet, lighting, portions of the electrical system, exterior site improvements such as sidewalks and landscaping, can often be depreciated over 5, 7 or 15 years, rather than over 27.5 or 39 years.

By using cost segregation, more depreciation is received in the earlier years of the investment which can effectively eliminate most of the income and significantly reduce or eliminate altogether the impact of any tax associated with UDFI.

Since depreciation is a paper-loss, in effect, it shelters the actual cash flow from taxation but does not diminish the cash received. If more losses are generated than income, the losses may be carried forward to offset any income recognized in future years.

Depreciation reduces the original basis, the original acquisition cost of the asset. When the property is sold, the IRS requires that a taxpayer pay tax on the gain realized between the sales price of the asset and its depreciated adjusted basis. On any debt-financed property the gain is allocated between depreciation recapture and long-term gain on sale, if the asset is held for longer than one year. Depreciation recapture is taxed at 25 percent.

Any losses that are not used to offset income are known as suspended losses and may be used to offset any gain on the sale of the asset. If the property is held for more than a year, any gain on the sale over the amount allocated for depreciation recapture is taxed at the capital gains rate on that portion of the gain related to the UDFI.

Review Questions

1. Real estate is one of the most common investments made by Self-Directed retirement plan investors.

   A. True
   B. False

2. Self-directed IRAs and 401(k)s may invest in all types of real estate, including residential and commercial properties.

   A. True
   B. False

3. When purchasing a property with a self-directed IRA or 401(k), all of the following statements are true except:

   A. Real estate owned by a retirement plan must always be held for investment.
   B. All income derived from the property should be paid directly to the retirement plan.
   C. All of the funds due at the purchase must be paid by the account owner and not the retirement plan.
   D. The retirement plan must be listed on the purchase contract as the buyer.

4. When purchasing a real estate property with a self-directed IRA or 401(k), all of the following statements are true except:

   A. The IRA or 401(k) owner is a disqualified person to his or her own retirement account and cannot pay expenses to the property with personal funds.
   B. The purchase contract cannot be assigned from a disqualified person (e.g., the IRA or 401(k) owner) to a retirement plan.
   C. Any earnest money deposit made for the purchase of the property should be paid by the retirement plan not the account owner.
   D. The assignment of a contract between an IRA and a disqualified person is NOT a per se prohibited transaction.

5. Which of the following statement is false?

   A. A self-directed IRA can obtain a loan to purchase real estate.
   B. A self-directed IRA owner can personally guarantee a loan for the IRA.
   C. Any loan obtained by a self-directed IRA to purchase real estate must be a non-recourse loan.
   D. A non-recourse loan is a loan where the lender's sole recourse in the event of default is to foreclose and take the property back.

6. If a self-directed IRA or 401(k) is going to be on title to real property with other owners, then the form of ownership must be:

    A. As a sole proprietor
    B. As a corporation
    C. As a general partner
    D. As a tenant in common

7. When managing an IRA or 401(k) investment assets, the IRA owner should limit his or her activities to administrative and investment oversight tasks.

    A. True
    B. False

8. Which of the following is a prohibited management action by the owner of a self-directed IRA or 401(k)?

    A. Making decisions as to the property manager or tenants
    B. Setting terms for the lease or other legal agreements
    C. Receiving rental income in the owner's personal account
    D. Visiting the property and overseeing repairs and maintenance

9. A self-directed IRA or 401(k) may **NOT** invest in real property that is being developed or purchased to flip for a profit.

    A. True
    B. False

10. When owning real estate with a self-directed IRA or 401(k), which of the following statements is correct?

    A. The contract and deed should be in the name of the IRA or 401(k).
    B. The self-directed IRA or 401(k) account owner should refrain from using personal funds to purchase the property.
    C. If the self-directed IRA or 401(k) obtains a loan to purchase the property, the loan should be nonrecourse.
    D. All of the above

Section Seven
Real Estate Investment Alternatives

Objectives

- **To discuss residential real estate investments in self-directed retirement accounts**
- **To discuss commercial real estate investments in self-directed retirement accounts**
- **To discuss other types of real estate-related investments in self-directed retirement accounts**

Residential Real Estate

Definition

Residential real estate is defined as single-family homes, manufactured homes, stationary mobile homes, building lots and land zoned for residential use, duplexes, triplexes, fourplexes. Anything over four units is considered multifamily and is usually classified as commercial real estate.

Acquisition

These types of properties are generally acquired from people advertising their property for sale, either by For Sale By Owner (FSBO) or through a real estate agent who is licensed with a state agency, affiliated with the National Association of Realtors, and with a local board of Realtors. Realtors generally advertise the properties they have listed for sale through a Multiple Listing Service, a cooperative advertising service showing all the residential and, in some cases, commercial properties for sale. In addition to these two sources, financial institutions may also be selling, through their Real Estate or REO (Real Estate Other) department, the properties they have acquired by foreclosure or through a short sale for properties which are in default where the value of the asset is less than the amount of the mortgage.

Investment Amount

The amount required to invest varies greatly depending on whether the property is leveraged (with debt) or unleveraged (without debt). On an unleveraged-basis, the amount could be as low as $20,000 to $30,000 for a used mobile home and could range as high as $600,000 or more for a fourplex. On a leveraged-basis, a lender usually requires 20 to 30 percent as a cash down payment and then will lend the balance, depending on the creditworthiness of the borrower. Since SDIRAs cannot personally guarantee the loan, there are some lenders who provide nonrecourse financing. HUD homes may be obtained for as little as 3.5 percent in a cash down payment. HUD homes are financed using an FHA loan. Non-HUD homes are financed using a conventional loan obtained through a bank, credit union, or mortgage company. These loans are usually financed by the lender and then sold to Fannie Mae or Freddie Mac on the secondary mortgage market. When economic times are bad, financial institutions may liquidate their asset portfolio by offering deep discounts from the standard fair market value or they may permit the property to be acquired using a short sale where the lender discounts the sale price below the mortgage amount it shows on its books.

Due Diligence

This usually consists of determining that the zoning of the property is correct, that there are no liens or encumbrances on the property, and that there are no environmental or governmental issues, such as an assessment from a special improvement district. A complete inspection of the physical property is also advisable. Licensed home inspectors will thoroughly evaluate the condition of the property and write up a formal report.

Factors When Buying

One of the most important factors when purchasing residential property is confirming that the price you are paying for the property does not exceed its fair market value. This is accomplished through a licensed appraiser. Other factors to consider may include whether or not the seller is willing to carry back seller financing or other financing options available. For older homes, it is imperative to confirm no environmental issues like the presence of asbestos or lead-based paint exist. Rectifying these conditions may be costly.

Financial Analysis

Financial analysis consists of determining the total cost to acquire the property, including the cost of any repairs, financing costs, and closing expenses. Once the actual cost of the project has been determined, evaluate the market to determine the rents that can be received or the sales price. If holding the property, there will be ongoing expenses such as property taxes, utilities, management and maintenance expenses. Additionally, money should be set aside in a reserve account to maintain the asset. Some reports that may help in analyzing a property is a Comparative Market Analysis (CMA) or a Broker's Price Opinion (BPO), both of which are usually performed by a realtor.

Management

An owner can manage the property themselves or they can hire professional property management who will manage and lease the property for a fee. For rentals, a formal application should be used, and prospective tenants should share past rental history, verify employment and perform a criminal background check. Also, pull a credit report and check for any payment delinquencies. The wrong tenant could take months to evict while they live rent free and damage the property.

Commercial Real Estate

Definition

Commercial property refers to buildings or land intended to generate a profit, either from capital gains or rental income. Residential multifamily property, containing more than four units, also qualifies as commercial property. Other commercial properties include office buildings, industrial property, medical centers, hotels, malls, retail stores, shopping centers and farm land.

Acquisition

These properties are usually listed for sale through a commercial real estate agent who works for a commercial brokerage company. Some of the more well-known national commercial brokerages are Coldwell Banker Commercial, CB Richard Ellis (also known as CBRE), Commerce CRG, NAI, Marcus & Millichap, Grubb & Ellis, and RE/MAX. These properties are generally listed on a commercial multiple listing service such as LoopNet.com or CoStar.com.

Build-to-Suit

A national credit tenant is a publicly-traded corporation that has strong credit and who operates either on a corporate basis or through franchisees or operating agreements the businesses that occupy the buildings. Some examples are Family Dollar, AutoZone, O'Reilly Auto Parts, Tractor Supply and Walgreen's. A builder/developer constructs the building and leases it to the national credit tenant on a long-term basis. The builder/developer forms an LLC and arranges for self-directed IRAs or other investors to participate in the ownership of the asset.

Investment Amount

The investment amount varies depending on the type and size of the project. One of the best ways for smaller investors who want to own commercial real estate is to participate in a Limited Liability Company or Limited Partnership that invites other members to participate and shares ownership on a pro rata basis. These investment contributions can be as small as $10,000.

Due Diligence

It is wise to hire a professional company that specializes in appraising and feasibility studies to handle the due diligence on a commercial building. A myriad of things need to be considered, from zoning, governmental and environmental issues to building maintenance, management and tenant leasing concerns.

Factors When Buying

Never purchase a commercial property without completing a market analysis and appraisal. For new construction, a feasibility study is also advisable.

Financial Analysis

When an appraisal is conducted on a commercial property, the appraiser uses three approaches to value: cost, market or sales comparison, and income. For income-producing properties, generally the most reliable estimate of value is the income approach. This approach considers the potential or current revenue that is being generated, and then determines the potential vacancy that exists or could exist, and then deducts comparable or historical operating expenses to determine the NOI before depreciation and debt service. The NOI is then divided by a capitalization rate to arrive at a projected value. Several methods for determining a capitalization rate exist, but the most common method is through market comparison. One method of calculating the capitalization rate is to divide the annual NOI by the value, sales price or cost of the asset. An appraiser generally knows the sales price of similar type commercial properties that have sold recently and what their net operating income has been. Most capitalization rates for commercial properties run between six and ten percent, depending on the type of property, risk of ownership, and the anticipated income stream. Once the capitalization rate is known for a particular property type, it can be divided into the NOI to determine its value. Small changes in the capitalization rate can make big changes in value, so it is important to have reliable data. The lower the capitalization rate, the higher the value because the cap rate is the denominator in the valuation equation.

Management

Because management and maintenance issues can be complex on a commercial project, it is highly recommended that a professional management company handle the management and maintenance issues. The management company is usually paid a percentage of the gross revenue collected to perform the management services.

International Real Estate

As international boundaries open up, investing in cross-border real estate is becoming an exciting option for some buyers. Several important things should be considered when investing in international real estate.

Only invest in properties that have a clean record. Any evidence of property disputes, such as multiple claimants or that the property has been under ownership of the government or a law enforcement agency, should strictly be avoided.

Hire professional, local counsel plus an international team to document the legal ownership of the property and to determine whether a foreigner can obtain clear title to the property. Improper legal evidence to claims over the property generally indicates false ownership or even forced ownership.

Before investing, decide on what is expected from the investment. Will the property be used as a post-retirement home, rental income, a holiday getaway, or a new home? Location is vital to maintain property value. Talk to several real estate agents in the country and do homework on the area.

Foreign nationals will encounter laws that restrict what they are allowed to invest in and what they can do with the property. Rights of purchase vary from country to country.

Check on the country's immigration restrictions. Each country has its own regulations and restrictions which specify the parameters that must be met to apply for permission to immigrate. The basic guidelines nearly all countries use for screening applicants are: 1) Do the two countries recognize each other, 2) Do you have a criminal history, and 3) Are you healthy?

Farm Real Estate

Purchasing a farm or ranch is much different from purchasing any other type of real estate because a buyer is not only purchasing real estate but is also buying a business to operate. Some buyers choose to either hire people to work the land for them or they rent the entire farm to an experienced operator who then pays the owner rent for the use of the land.

Although experienced real estate agents can find a farm or ranch to own, there is also a plethora of information available on the internet. Regardless of the method used to find the property, it is imperative to hire an experienced analyst to assist with the evaluation and acquisition. Because farming and agricultural management are so vital to the United States, many government programs offer grants, loans and other types of money to farm owners. The United States Department of Agriculture oversees many of these loan programs.

Real Estate Options

A real estate option is a legal document that gives the holder the exclusive right to buy or not to buy a property. While the option is valid, no one else can buy or sell the property during the option term. Options work best in markets where conditions are changing rapidly.

For example, a farmer owns property along a major roadway where a developer has announced that it will build a 1,000-home residential community. The farmer's land is zoned for agricultural uses. Meet with the farmer and persuade him to sell you an option on the property for a period of one year. During that time, with his permission, invest the additional capital to rezone his property to a commercial use, knowing that retailers and other commercial users will be looking for land near the new residential community. Immediately upon rezone, sell the property for a substantially higher price or exercise the option and keep the property for future development. Either way, an owner has risked a relatively small amount of money for the opportunity of making a large amount of money.

Options are a tricky business. One can either win a substantial sum or lose an entire investment. Even then, unforeseen market forces may thwart best efforts. For instance, maybe the highway department decides to put an island in the middle of the road making it impossible to access the property from certain directions. Options are not for the faint hearted, nor are they appropriate for the novice investor. They are best left to experienced real estate developers who understand market trends and know how to evaluate locations.

Promissory Notes[1]

As an investment, a self-directed retirement account may lend money to a borrower. The IRA or 401(k) is the lender and the party receiving the loan funds is the borrower. The borrower cannot be a disqualified person. A loan to a disqualified person (e.g., the IRA owner or certain family members) would result in a prohibited transaction. IRC §4975(c)(1)(B).

The loan must be evidenced by a written loan document--such as a promissory note--and may be secured by real estate or other assets or may be unsecured. A promissory note is the legal obligation between the IRA (the lender) and the borrower. Typically, it is only signed by the borrower. The terms of the promissory note will indicate the amount loaned, the interest rate charged, the periodic payment amounts, and the due date of the loan.

Once the promissory note has been prepared and signed by the borrower, the IRA owner will instruct the IRA custodian to fund the loan. If the note is secured, the property will be pledged as collateral for the loan and a deed of trust or mortgage will be recorded against the property. A deed of trust or mortgage is a lien recorded against the title to the property. It protects the lender (the IRA). Should the borrower default, the IRA may foreclose and force a sale of the property to satisfy the amount owed on the promissory note.

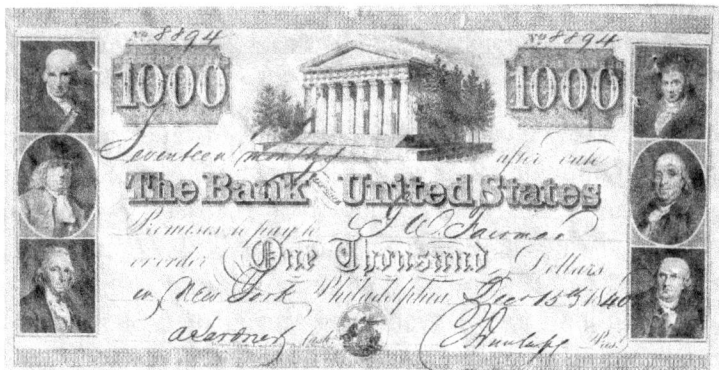

---

[1]Mat Sorensen, *The Self Directed IRA Handbook* (SoKoh Publishing, LLC, 2014), 126-137. Note: The information contained in the Promissory Note section was taken from Mat Sorensen's book. However, in most instances, it has been paraphrased for brevity rather than being quoted verbatim. The Promissory Note Terms & Checklist was quoted verbatim.

Promissory notes have various payment terms. They may require monthly payments or a one lump-sum payment at the end of the note term. They may be amortized over a number of years or paid on an interest only basis. Usually, the note is due prior to it being fully amortized, which then requires a balloon payment at the time it is due. At the "balloon date," all accrued interest and principal are due.

Promissory note payments may be made directly to the note holder (the lender) or they may be made to a third-party payment servicer known as an escrow company. The escrow company or service processor receives the payment, catalogs the payment and deducts a small processing fee before sending it to the lender. The benefit of using an escrow company is that they are in the business of keeping track of payments and due dates. So, if the borrower misses a payment, they notify the lender and begin tacking on late fees and penalty interest until the borrower is current. If the borrower continues to miss payments, they assist the lender through the foreclosure process. They also keep track of balloon payment dates.

The IRA owner should never personally receive the payments for the IRA. The IRA owner is not permitted to deal directly with the income or assets of his or her IRA. IRC §49875(c)(1)(E).

The interest rate charged on the promissory note must be commercially reasonable and must be based on an arm's-length transaction at fair market value to be in compliance with the Exclusive Benefit Rule. IRC §408(a). Interest rates that are excessively low or excessively high are suspect and may raise compliance questions with the custodian. For example, in real estate, an annual interest rate of one percent is not commercially available nor is a rate of 30 percent commercially reasonable. It is likely that both would violate the Exclusive Benefit Rule.

When drafting a promissory note, rely on a good attorney or title company. There are laws that apply to loans which the typical IRA owner needs to comply with. California, for instance, has a usury law that restricts the interest charged on a loan to a maximum rate of 10 percent annually. Calif. Const. Art. 15. California's 10 percent usury interest-rate restriction contains numerous exceptions, such as an exception when the loan is brokered and secured by real property. These exceptions require strict compliance to avoid violating usury laws.

Promissory notes may be secured or unsecured. A secured promissory note is where the borrower pledges certain assets (e.g., real property) to the lender as collateral for the loan. If the borrower defaults, the lender can sell the collateral to satisfy payment of the amounts owed. With a secured promissory note, the borrower permits the lender to place a lien (depending on the state, it is called a mortgage or deed of trust) against the real property.

Either a mortgage or a deed of trust is a lien against the real property. Under a mortgage, the lender must go to court to enforce a default, whereas, under a deed of trust, the lender can foreclose after giving certain notices to the borrower without having to get court approval. Always work with a title company and/or local real estate attorney to draft the promissory note and to record a lien against the property.

In most cases, the custodian will require that a real estate attorney or title company be involved in the transaction. They will also require a lender instruction letter to be issued to the title company handling the transaction. The instruction letter to the title company will include conditions that must be met before loan funds are released to the borrower.

An unsecured promissory note is a loan that is not secured by any real or personal property of the borrower. An unsecured promissory note is more risky than a secured promissory note. It is imperative to analyze the borrower's ability to repay the loan if an unsecured promissory note is used. Secured promissory notes are preferred to unsecured notes because the lender has collateral against which to collect in the event of a default.

If the promissory note is secured by personal property rather than real property, a security agreement and a UCC-1 filing are used. The security agreement is a contract between the borrower and the lender. It outlines the property being secured by the promissory note and states the process by which the IRA (lender) may take possession of the property upon an event of default. The UCC-1 filing is a form document signed by the borrower and typically filed with the Secretary of State (or state corporation division depending on the state) where the property and/or the borrower are located. The UCC-1 filing should identify the borrower, the loan, the secured party (e.g., the IRA), and the property subject to the UCC-1 lien (e.g., equipment VIN, stock/unit share numbers, or other pertinent property description).

Promissory Note Terms and Checklist

At a minimum, a promissory note should include the following terms:

- Amount loaned
- Date of loan
- Monthly payment amount and due date, or lump-sum due date
- Interest rate being charged and type of rate. Annual, simple, or compounded interest, etc. including an amortization table of the interest and payments is helpful to clarify the interest being charged and the payments due.
- Name of borrower. If the borrower is a company, it is helpful to obtain the personal guarantee of the owner(s) of the company.

- The IRA should be listed as the lender (e.g., ABC Trust Company FBO Sally Jones IRA).
- Default clause, state what constitutes default.
- Acceleration clause, which allows the lender to call the entire note due if the borrower defaults on a payment.
- Attorney's and collection feed provisions, allowing the lender ("IRA") to recoup expenses incurred in collecting on a defaulted loan.
- Place of payment. To a payment processor or escrow company or to the IRA custodian directly.
- Late payment fee/penalty
- Description of collateral securing the loan (e.g., real estate or equipment) if the loan is secured. A deed of trust or mortgage should be included when the loan is secured by real property. If the loan is secured by equipment or other personal property, the loan is typically secured by a UCC-1 filing.
- If the loan is secured by real estate, obtain a title insurance policy in favor of the IRA (lender) protecting the title position of the deed of trust/mortgage.
- If the loan is secured by real estate, issue lender instructions to the title company or attorney handling the closing.
- Obtain a loan application from the borrower and collect the borrower's SSN, date of birth, address, employer, income, and assets. This information is vitally important in the event of default as it will assist in collection efforts. It is also helpful in the event that the loan is cancelled as a 1099-C should be issued to the uncollectible borrower.
- Loan document drafting fees and title insurance costs, which protect the lender (IRA), should be paid by the borrower at closing. This is the customary practice of lenders.
- Signature of the borrower and any guarantors to the loan. The lender to a loan typically does not sign the loan.

Private Mortgage Financing Alternatives

A mortgage is a legal document that evidences the owner of real estate transfers to the lender, a security interest in the real estate to secure the repayment of a debt, evidenced by a mortgage note or promissory note. Mortgages and deeds of trust are different types of security instruments lenders use to secure their interest in real estate when they lend money to a borrower to purchase real estate. The state where the financing is taking place determines whether a mortgage or deed of trust is used. Many times these two terms are used interchangeably. To determine which security instrument is best in a situation, contact a local real estate attorney.

A private mortgage is similar to a bank mortgage, except that it is provided through an individual or group of investors rather than a financial institution or government agency such as Fannie Mae or Freddie Mac.

Self-directed IRAs may provide financing for real estate either individually or in participation through a group of investors. Listed are some examples of the type of financing that a self-directed IRA may engage in:

Home Mortgages (First Mortgages, Second Mortgages and Home Equity Loans)

A first mortgage is recorded with the county in which the loan is made, in first position against the property. This mortgage has to be paid first in the event of a sale or default. A second mortgage is in second position, etc. In the event of a foreclosure, the second mortgage holder will receive no proceeds from the sale of the real estate until the first mortgage holder has been completely paid. A first, second or third mortgage does not designate the type of loan being obtained, only the security position in which the loan has been recorded.

Construction Loans

A construction loan is a short-term, non-permanent loan for financing the cost of construction. Most construction loans last six to nine months, but may last longer depending upon the complexity of the project. These loans are also interest-only loans, meaning the borrower does not pay down the loan amount but simply makes interest payments during the life of the loan.

Bridge Loans

A bridge loan is interim financing for an individual or business until permanent financing can be obtained. Money from the permanent financing is generally used to take out the bridge loan. Bridge loans are typically more expensive than conventional financing to compensate for the additional risk of the loan. They typically have higher interest rates, points (also known as loan origination fees) and other costs that are charged to the borrower.

Permanent or Take-Out Loans

A permanent, long-term mortgage loan is designed to refinance or take out an interim short-term loan, such as a construction or bridge loan. Investing in private mortgages through a self-directed IRA can be profitable if a few guidelines are followed:

1. ***Always determine the value of the real estate.*** The most conventional approach to determining value is by obtaining an appraisal from a licensed appraiser. Other methods for determining value might be through a comparative market analysis or BPO obtained from an experienced real estate agent.

2. ***Establish the appropriate loan-to-value ratio for the type of loan provided.*** Typically, someone in first mortgage position will have a 65 to 75 percent loan-to-value ratio. The loan-to-value ratio is determined by dividing the amount of the loan by the value of the asset. These loans are in the most secure position and usually charge the lowest interest rate. Someone in second mortgage position may lend the difference between 70 and 90 percent loan-to-value and charge a higher interest rate for taking more risk. They may also require additional collateral from the borrower. In both instances, the lender usually requires a personal guarantee from the borrower.

3. ***Always do homework.*** Get a legal description of the property and confirm it is indeed the real estate you are lending on. A survey can confirm the legal description. Check the title to insure that you are in first or second position. Check the borrower's credit to confirm that you are lending to a reputable borrower. Validate the means of repayment. If the borrower defaults on the loan, foreclosure is a time-consuming process, so make sure are confident the borrower has the ability to repay the loan. Laws regarding mortgage default and foreclosure differ from state to state, so understanding your state's rules and having a good real estate attorney are necessary in any foreclosure process.

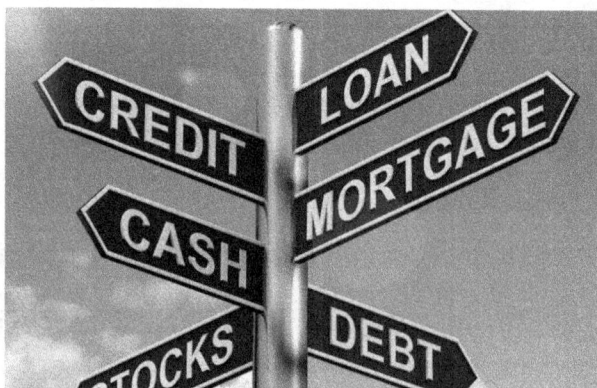

Funding private mortgages through a self-directed IRA can be an excellent way to grow a retirement account. It is not uncommon for private mortgages to achieve returns of 10 to 16 percent interest. An investor should surround themselves with good professionals. A good accountant, real estate attorney, real estate agent and mortgage broker are essential team members.

Participating Loans

A participating loan is a hybrid loan which incorporates elements of a traditional takeout loan but also provides participation in the cash flow during the holding period of the property and participation in the appreciation of the property at the time of sale. It carries benefits similar to ownership without triggering UDFI. Usually with a participating loan, the money is loaned to the builder/developer who uses the money to meet the equity requirement of the lender. The loan is single purpose treated as unsecured to the property, but is secured by the LLC owning the asset. Thus, if the builder/developer defaults on the participating loan, the lender assumes control of the LLC. The participating loan usually has a lower stated rate but receives a fairly high percentage of the cash flow and net cash on the sale of the asset.

Tax Deed & Tax Liens

Definition: When property owners fail to pay the required property tax assessed on real property, the property may be auctioned and sold at a real property tax sale, though real property is not always sold at tax sales. Some states engage in the sale of deeds to real property to recoup losses from delinquent property taxes. Other states engage in the sale of liens against real property recoup the losses.

The purchase of a tax deed is significantly different from the purchase of a tax lien. States that engage in the sale of tax deeds are considered tax deed states. The winning bidder bids for immediate possession of deed and title to a property. A tax deed is issued or assigned in return for the payment of unpaid real property taxes as well as associated penalties, interest, and costs of the tax sale.

States that engage in the sale of tax liens are considered tax lien states. The tax sale initiates a process or system by which an investor pays the delinquent tax on behalf of the property owner. The property owner is then given an opportunity to repay the investor or be forced to relinquish title and deed to the property in the future. A certificate that indicates payment of the tax lien is issued or assigned in return for the payment of unpaid real property taxes as well as associated penalties, interest, and costs of the tax sale.

States that give the previous property owner an opportunity to redeem the property for the newly established owner are called hybrid tax deed states. States that do not provide the previous property owner the opportunity to redeem a property and regain ownership are considered to be pure tax deed states. In tax lien states, no deed or title transfers are executed as a direct result of a tax sale. The winning bidder purchases a tax lien certificate, and a parcel of property is used to secure the lien. The delinquent property owner retains ownership of the property and is allowed an opportunity to redeem the tax lien held against the property. Different tax lien states have differing systems for recouping delinquent real estate tax. The sale of tax lien certificates is strictly an offer to investors to collect the delinquent property tax. If the property owner fails to redeem a tax lien certificate during the redemption period, the deed to the property is offered for sale at a second auction.

Hybrid Tax Deed States	Pure Tax Deed States	Tax Lien States
Connecticut	Alaska	Alabama
Delaware	Arkansas	Arizona
Georgia	California	Colorado
Guam	Idaho	District of Columbia
Hawaii	Kansas	Florida
Louisiana	Maine	Illinois
Massachusetts	Michigan	Indiana
Pennsylvania	Minnesota	Iowa
Rhode Island	Nevada	Kentucky
Tennessee	New Hampshire	Maryland
Texas	New Mexico	Michigan
	New York	Mississippi
	North Carolina	Missouri
	Ohio	Montana
	Oregon	Nebraska
	Utah	New Jersey
	Virginia	North Dakota
	Washington	Oklahoma
	Wisconsin	Oregon
		Puerto Rico
		South Carolina
		South Dakota
		Vermont
		West Virginia
		Wyoming

In tax deed states, the winning bidder at a tax sale purchases ownership to a property as specified by a tax deed. The bidder becomes the property owner upon payment of the delinquent tax amount and any other costs and fees assessed against the property. In some tax deed states, the previous property owner is given an opportunity to redeem the property from the newly established owner. The redemption period varies among the states, but generally ranges from six months to two years.

A tax lien certificate is a real estate document that services as evidence of indebtedness against a parcel of real estate. When tax lien certificates are sold, the parcel of real estate serves as collateral to secure the purchase of the tax lien certificate. Different states refer to the Tax Lien Certificate by various names that include the following:

- Tax Lien Certificate
- Tax Sale Certificate
- Tax Sale Receipt
- Tax Lien
- Certificate of Delinquency
- Certificate of Purchase
- Receipt Showing the Amount Paid
- Receipt for the Purchase Money
- Tax Claim
- Tax Certificate

Most tax deed states hold periodic delinquent property tax sales. Depending upon the taxing jurisdiction of the state, sales may be held as often as weekly, or the range of sales may extend to monthly, quarterly, or biannually. Most tax lien states, on the other hand, hold annual property tax sales. The annual sale is a process of auctioning available tax lien certificates to the public.

One of the disadvantages of tax sales for investors is that most are held annually. In addition, many states hold their annual tax sales on the same day, making it impossible for investors to be present at multiple auctions. This limits the number of opportunities that investors have to invest in tax lien certificates. Since most tax sales are only offered annually, it can be difficult to reinvest the funds received from redemption amounts in new tax liens. A new trend for some municipalities is engaging in online auctions.

Real Estate Investment Trusts

A REIT is a company that raises money through its stockholders to acquire, and in many cases, operate income-producing commercial real estate. Some REITs also engage in financing real estate. In order for a company to qualify as a REIT, it must comply with certain strict provisions within the Internal Revenue Code. For example, at least 75 percent of the company's total assets must be invested in real estate, and at least 75 percent of its gross income must come from rents from real property or interest from mortgages. REITs are required to pass at least 90 percent of taxable income to stockholders.

REITs were created by Congress in 1960, in part to make investments in large-scale, income-producing real estate assets more accessible to smaller investors. Congress determined that a way for individual investors to invest in large scale commercial properties was the same way they invest in other industries, through the pooling of capital to purchase equity. In the same way as shareholders can benefit by owning stocks of other corporations, the stockholders of a REIT earn a pro-rata share of the economic benefits that are derived from the production of income and potential appreciation of commercial real estate ownership.

Two Primary Types of REITs	
Publicly Traded REITs	Traded REITs or listed REITs are registered with the U.S. Securities & Exchange Commission and shares are bought and sold on a national stock exchange just like traditional exchange-traded stocks or funds. While they can provide many of the benefits associated with direct real estate investing, such income producing dividends, these Traded REITs are subject to the same market volatility and fluctuations of any stock or fund that is traded on a national stock exchange. As a result, investors who invest in Traded REITs should anticipate some correlation to the stock market and the potential for more volatility due to fluctuations in the stock market.
Non-Traded REITs	Non-Traded or Non-Listed REITs are also registered with the U.S. Securities & Exchange Commission. However, shares of these REITs are not publicly traded on any national stock exchange and thus are less correlated to the stock market. The real estate behaves more like a hard asset. As a result, investors' returns are based more upon the performance of the real estate owned by the REIT and have less outside influence from the stock market. Non-Traded REITs, however, do not offer the liquidity of a Publicly Traded REIT. Due to the lack of liquidity of Non-Traded REITs, certain income and net worth requirements must be met in order to qualify for this type of investment.

What Types of Properties do REITs Purchase?

REITs invest in a variety of property types, requiring different strategy in the types of properties acquired and the objectives of those properties. Property types include office building, shopping centers, healthcare facilities, apartments, hotels, warehouses, and self-storage facilities. Most REITs specialize in one property type. However, some REITs are a hybrid. These acquire multiple property types to achieve a certain objective. REITs will also differ with respect to acquisition objectives.

General REIT Benefits

REITs offer the distinct advantage of greater diversification through investing in a portfolio of properties rather than a single property. They also provide management by experienced real estate professionals. REITs are designed to provide investors with steady income in the form of monthly or quarterly dividends, as well as growth potential in the appreciation of the properties owned by the REIT.

REITs may also help investors diversify their assets and overall portfolio allocation. While most investors have substantial holdings of stocks, bonds and mutual funds, for many investors, real estate is overlooked. Many investors feel that in order to invest in real estate, they must have substantial amounts of capital, assume new debt and loans and be experienced at managing real estate. REITs can help alleviate some of these requirements as they offer low minimum investments, they do not require investors to acquire a loan and the properties are managed by experienced real estate professionals. Although diversification does not guarantee against losses, a Non-Traded REIT can help diversify a portfolio that is heavily concentrated in stocks or other traded securities, by spreading out the risk and allowing investors to incorporate real estate into their portfolio.

Tax advantages are often passed along to investors in REITs, which are not taxed at the corporate level. Some stockholders can also reduce their overall tax burden with property depreciation benefits that REITs may create. Investors are always encouraged to seek a tax professional in determining the tax benefits of a REIT as it relates to their personal tax planning.

General REIT Risks

- No guarantee regarding future performance, and upon the sale or distribution of the REIT's assets, stockholders may receive less than their initial investment
- Real estate values can increase or decrease based on economic factors, including interest rates, laws, operating expenses, insurance costs, unemployment, and tenant turnover
- Publicly Traded REITs are subject to stock market volatility
- Non-Traded REITs do not have a public market and may lack liquidity and transferability
- Distributions from REITs may be paid from offering proceeds, the sale of assets, or borrowed funds
- Fees are associated with investments in a REIT, and those fees may affect the overall performance of the investment

Real Estate Leases

Purchasing a residential property and leasing it is one of the safest investments in the real estate business which provides attractive returns. Two examples of residential rental real estate are condominium rentals and model home rentals.

Condominiums fit between apartment rentals and single family homes. They are similar to apartments in that they are usually part of a multifamily project. They generally have the same type of amenities as upscale apartment communities, but they cater to a higher income group and someone who wants ownership privileges but doesn't want the obligation of maintaining the grounds and common area. Some people prefer condominiums because they typically have professional management and security. A condominium owner also enjoys being able to leave his property unattended and know someone is keeping an eye on it and not letting the property deteriorate in their absence. Condominium owners belong to a homeowners association and pay monthly dues for maintenance of the common area.

Condominiums make attractive investments for investors who like residential real estate but want the advantages of income. By purchasing a condominium, an investor has the benefit of owning an income-producing investment plus the added advantage of professional property management. Rental rates for condominiums usually track the apartment rental market, but are significantly higher because the quality and class of tenant is usually better. Oftentimes, tenants are executives who are relocating to a community but want the benefit of getting acquainted with the area before choosing which neighborhood they would like to live in.

Another popular, but less available leasing option, is teaming up with a local residential builder and purchasing a model home which the builder leases back for a period of time while it is selling out the residential lots in a subdivision.

One of the primary benefits of leasing a model home to a local builder is that there is no concern that the property will become vacant or will not be well-maintained. Since the builder is using the property as its model home, it usually stays in pristine condition with little wear-and-tear on the facility.

Model homes are usually placed in strategic locations within the subdivision. If the project sells out quickly, it is likely the model home, which is generally the last home available, will sell out quickly. If the project sells out more slowly, the investor has the benefit of receiving monthly income for a longer period of time.

Since model homes are less prevalent than condominiums, it is more difficult to find one available for lease. In either case, both alternatives make excellent income-producing investments.

Build-To-Suits

One attractive investment option for SDIRAs is purchasing a newly constructed building from a developer/builder who has pre-arranged for the building to be leased on a long-term basis to a national credit tenant. A national credit tenant is a publicly-traded corporation that has strong credit and operates stores either on a national or regional basis. The stores may be owned and managed by the corporation itself or they may be owned and managed by a franchisee. Some examples of national credit tenants are Family Dollar, Dollar General, AutoZone, O'Reilly Auto Parts, Tractor Supply and Walgreen's.

Typically, the developer/builder forms a limited liability company which owns the building. The LLC is then owned by a group of SDIRA investors or TICs and the developer/builder. The equity capital is generally provided by the investment group and the developer/ builder obtains any financing and personally guarantees the loan, which enables the SDIRAs to invest without having any recourse debt, which is not permitted under IRS regulations.

Resources

IRS Publications for IRA and Small Business Plans	
IRS Publication 529	Miscellaneous Deductions
IRS Publication 550	Investment Income and Expenses
IRS Publication 560	Small Business Retirement Plans
IRS Publication 575	IRS Publication 575
IRS Publication 590	Individual Retirement Accounts
IRS Publication 3125	Information on IRA approved investments
IRC Section 4925	Disqualified Persons

Review Questions

1. A self-directed retirement account can purchase residential real estate including single-family homes, manufactured homes, stationary mobile homes, building lots, and land zoned for residential use.

    A. True
    B. False

2. All of the following are considered commercial real estate except:

    A. Office buildings
    B. Industrial property
    C. Hotels
    D. Single-family homes

3. When purchasing a commercial real estate property with a self-directed retirement account, you should do all of the following except:

    A. Perform due diligence on the property
    B. Hire an appraisal to be completed
    C. Obtain a feasibility study from a qualified professional company
    D. All of the above

4. International real estate CANNOT be purchased using self-directed retirement account funds.

    A. True
    B. False

5. A legal document that gives the holder the exclusive right to buy or not to buy a real estate property is called:

    A. A real estate option
    B. A real estate purchase contract
    C. A deed of trust
    D. A promissory note

6. A self-directed retirement account may NOT lend money to a borrower.

    A. True
    B. False

7. When lending money from a self-directed retirement account, all of the following statements are true except:

    A. The loan must be evidenced by a written loan document
    B. If the note is secured, the property will be pledged as collateral for the loan
    C. The retirement account owner should personally receive the payments
    D. The note payments can be made to either the note holder (the lender) or an escrow company

8. A hybrid loan that incorporates the elements of a traditional takeout loan but also provides participation in the cash flow of the property during the holding period is called:

    A. A home equity loan
    B. A construction loan
    C. A bridge loan
    D. A participating loan

9. A self-directed IRA or 401(k) may purchase which of the following?

    A. Tax deeds
    B. Tax liens
    C. Real estate investment trusts (REITs)
    D. All of the above

10. A company that raises money through its stockholders to acquire and operate income-producing commercial real estate is called:

    A. A self-directed IRA
    B. A real estate investment trust
    C. A self-directed 401(k)
    D. A pension plan

Appendix A
Individual K Plan Application

Mountain West IRA
The Ultimate Retirement Machine

INDIVIDUAL(K) PLAN

APPLICATION

10096 W. Fairview Ave., Ste. 160
Boise, ID 83704
P: (866) 377-3311 | F: (208) 376-4567

609 Court Street
Clearwater, FL 33756
P: (727) 222-4200 | F: (727) 447-4567

Mountain West IRA
The Ultimate Retirement Machine

**INDIVIDUAL(K) PLAN
APPLICATION**

10096 W. Fairview Ave., Ste. 160
Boise, ID 83704
Phone: (208) 377-3311
Fax: (208) 376-4567

For Office Use Only:
Retirement Account Administrator: _____ Mountain West IRA, Inc._____

Client account number:_____
An account number will be assigned by the administrator and will be mailed to you

Participant Information

Date of birth *(M/D/Y)*	Social Security Number *(Required)*	Email Address
	— —	

☐Mr. ☐Ms. ☐Mrs. ☐Dr. **Name** _____

Mailing Address: _____

CITY: _____ STATE: _____ ZIP: _____ COUNTY (Required): _____

Legal Address: _____

CITY: _____ STATE: _____ ZIP: _____ COUNTY (Required): _____

Contact Information

Home Phone #: _____ Cell Phone #: _____ Fax #: _____

Account Type (Please Complete 1. and 2.)

1. Employer Portion: ☐ Traditional   **2. Employee Portion:** ☐ Traditional   ☐ Roth

Marital Status: ☐Single ☐Married (see Consent of Spouse) ☐Widowed/Divorced   **How did you hear about us:** _____

Occupation (Required):_____ **Title (Required):**_____
(If retired, please list previous occupation)

Online Access/Notifications

Would you like to review your statements online?	Would you like to receive e-mail notifications of changes to your account?
☐YES ☐NO ($5 Paper Statement Fee Applies)	☐YES ☐NO

Entity Establishing Plan

Tax ID Number of Business	Legal Name of Business

Fund Your Account

How would you like to fund your account?

	Salary Deferral Contribution		Employer Profit Sharing Contribution		Transfer Contribution		Rollover Contribution		Direct Rollover Contribution
☐		☐		☐		☐		☐	
	Contribution for year_____		*Contribution for year_____*		*Transfer from an existing IRA or Employer Sponsored Plan*		*Take Receipt of the assets for up to 60 days before reinvesting in a new plan*		*Rollover from Employer Sponsored Plan*

Page 1 of 5

95

Mountain West IRA
The Ultimate Retirement Machine

**INDIVIDUAL(K) PLAN
APPLICATION**

10096 W. Fairview Ave., Ste. 160
Boise, ID 83704
Phone: (208)377-3311
Fax: (208)376-4567

Beneficiary Designation

Account Holder: _____ *I designate the following person(s) named below as my primary and/or Contingent Beneficiaries of my plan. If the Primary or Contingent box is not checked for a beneficiary, the beneficiary will be deemed to be a Primary Beneficiary. In the event of my death, the balance in the account shall be paid to the Primary Beneficiaries who survive me in equal shared (or in the specified shares, as indicated). If none of the Primary Beneficiaries survive me, the balance in the account shall be paid to the Contingent Beneficiaries whose survive me in equal shares (or in the specified shares, as indicated). If any Primary or Contingent Beneficiary does not survive me, such beneficiary's interest and the interest of such beneficiary's hairs shall terminate completely, and the share for any remaining Primary or Contingent Beneficiary shall be increased on a pro rata basis. If no Primary or Contingent Beneficiary survives me, the remaining balance in the account shall be distributed in accordance with the plan provisions to my estate.*

Primary   Contingent

☐   ☐

Name: _____ SSN: _____ Birthdate: _____

Address: _____ Relationship: _____

CITY: _____ STATE: _____ ZIP: _____ Share: _____%

Primary   Contingent

☐   ☐

Name: _____ SSN: _____ Birthdate: _____

Address: _____ Relationship: _____

CITY: _____ STATE: _____ ZIP: _____ Share: _____%

Primary   Contingent

☐   ☐

Name: _____ SSN: _____ Birthdate: _____

Address: _____ Relationship: _____

CITY: _____ STATE: _____ ZIP: _____ Share: _____%

Primary   Contingent

☐   ☐

Name: _____ SSN: _____ Birthdate: _____

Address: _____ Relationship: _____

CITY: _____ STATE: _____ ZIP: _____ Share: _____%

Primary   Contingent

☐   ☐

Name: _____ SSN: _____ Birthdate: _____

Address: _____ Relationship: _____

CITY: _____ STATE: _____ ZIP: _____ Share: _____%

Consent of Spouse
Only required if your spouse is not the primary beneficiary

I consent to the above Beneficiary Designation.

Signature of Spouse _____ **Date:** _____

(Note: Consent of the Participant's Spouse may be required in a community property or marital property state to effectively designate a beneficiary other than or in addition to the Participant's Spouse.) Disclaimer for Community and Marital Property States: The Participant's Spouse may have a property interest in the account and the right to dispose of the interest by will. Therefore, the Custodian disclaims any warranty as to the effectiveness of the Participant's beneficiary designation or as to the ownership of the account after the death of the Participant's Spouse. For additional information, please consult your legal advisor.

Mountain West IRA
The Ultimate Retirement Machine

INDIVIDUAL(K) PLAN APPLICATION

10096 W. Fairview Ave., Ste. 160
Boise, ID 83704
Phone: (208) 377-3311
Fax: (208) 376-4567
E-Mail: accounts@MWIRA.com

7. Fee Schedule

Participant Name:_____   Account No.:_____

RECORDKEEPING FEE (CHOOSE ONE)

☐ **Option One:** (Charged upon asset purchase/ then quarterly)
Quarterly Fee Based on Number of Investments

☐ **Option Two:** (Charged upon asset purchase/ then annually)
Annual Fee Based on Total Account Value

$75 Per Quarter Per Asset and/or Liability
(Plus Asset Transaction Processing Fees)

Asset Transaction Processing Fees:

Purchase, Sale, Exchange or Re-Registration of Assets or Liabilities:

Real Estate: $125
Non-Real Estate: $95

Total Account Value	Marginal Rate Multiplier	Annual Fees
$0-$24,999		$200
$25,000-$49,999	.01	$200-$450
$50,000-$99,999	.005	$450-$700
$100,000-$249,999	.00266	$700-$1,100
$250,000-$499,999	.0022	$1,100-$1,650
$500,000-$750,000	.0008	$1,650-$1,850
$750,000+	N/A	$1,850

Example: $125,000 account = ($700+($25,000 x .00266)) = $766.50

Purchase, Sale, Exchange or Re-Registration of Assets or Liabilities:
Real Estate: $0
Non-Real Estate: $0

NOTE: If a Recordkeeping Fee Option is not selected, fees will be based on Option Two – Account Value. Recordkeeping Fees are not prorated or refundable. If your IRA holds only uninvested cash, a quarterly fee of $25.00 will be assessed.

ALL ACCOUNTS INCLUDE AT NO CHARGE

- Online Account Access
- Annual Tax Reporting

- Annual Account Summary Statements
- Required Minimum Distributions by Check
- Access to Regular Education/Networking Events

PROCESSING FEES

- Account Establishment: $50 **(Due when application is rcvd)**
- Roth Conversion or Re-characterization: $50
- Recordkeeping Fee Option Change: $50
- Wire Transfers: $25
- Cashiers or Other Official Bank Check: $10
- ACH Transfers or Trust Checks: $5; Expedited Processing: $5
- Returned Items or Stop Payment Request: $35

- Overnight Mail: $35
- Individual (k) Plan Document Fee: $300/year; Plan EIN: $50
- Paper Statements: $5 (Electronic stmts provided at no cost)
- Special Services and Legal Research: Up to $150/hour
- Expedited Investment Processing: $95
- Partial Outgoing Transfer: $95 plus processing fees
- Full Account Termination: $150 plus processing fees

FEE PAYMENT METHOD: ☐ FUND FROM ACCOUNT   ☐ CREDIT/DEBIT CARD   ☐ CHECK*
☐ BILL THIRD PARTY_____Billing party must be
pre-arranged through Mountain West IRA. If, for any reason, third party is unwilling or unable to pay fees, the account holder is responsible.

NAME ON CARD:_____   BILLING ADDRESS:_____

CITY:_____   STATE:_____ZIP CODE:_____

CARD NUMBER:_____   EXPIRATION DATE:_____

SECURITY CODE:_____   SIGNATURE:_____
We will automatically bill your credit card. Your total charges will appear on your electronic credit card payment receipt.   You may cancel this automatic billing authorization at any time by contacting us.

If an invoice on your account is unpaid for 30 days and funds are unavailable in the account, the credit/debit card on file for the account will be charged.
-Penalty for Late Payment of Quarterly Fees: $25   -Penalty for Late Payment of Annual Fees: $75

Recordkeeping fees are not prorated and are normally withdrawn from your undirected funds unless you submit payment directly prior to the due date by check, credit or debit card. Fees paid from your account will be reflected on your statement. You may also prepay fees by check, credit or debit card. *Accounts paying fees by check, or those carrying a $0 cash balance, must be paid in advance and are required to maintain a $500 credit with the administrator. If there are insufficient undirected funds in your account, we may liquidate other assets in your account to pay for such fees after a 30 day notification, in accordance with your Plan and Trust Disclosure. You agree and direct the Administrator that your un-directed cash is placed in government insured instruments, including FDIC insured banks, unless we are otherwise directed by you. Custodial fees are part of the plan and trust disclosure. In accordance with your Account Application, this Fee Schedule is part of your Agreement with Administrator. If a Recordkeeping Fee Option is not selected, fees will be based on "Option Two – Account Value".

Signature: _____   Date: _____

Individual(k) Plan Application

Appointment: I appoint Mountain West IRA, Inc. to be the Record Keeper for my Individual 401(k) account with the employer listed on this application.

I acknowledge that I am (**initial the appropriate status**):

_____The employer and that I am the Trustee and Plan Administrator of the Individual (k) plan and that I can appoint a successor Trustee or Plan Administrator.
_____The spouse of the employer and I acknowledge that the employer is the Trustee and Plan Administrator of my account.
_____A partner of the employer named in this application and that the employer is the Trustee and Plan Administrator.

Written direction shall be construed so as to include facsimile signature. The account is established for the exclusive benefit of the Account holder for his/her beneficiaries.

Responsibility for Tax Consequences: I assume all responsibility for any tax consequences and penalties that may result from making contributions to, transactions with and distributions from my Account. I am authorized and of legal age to establish this Account and make investment purchases permitted under the Plan Agreement offered by the Record Keeper. I assume complete responsibility for: 1) Determining that I am eligible for an Account transaction that I direct the Record Keeper to make on my behalf; 2) Insuring that all contributions I make are within the limits set forth by the tax laws; 3) The tax consequences of any contribution (including rollover contributions and distributions).

I certify under penalties of perjury: 1) that I have provided you with my correct Social Security or Tax I.D. Number; and 2) that I am not subject to backup withholding because: a) I am exempt from backup withholding; or b) I have not been notified by the Internal Revenue Service (IRS) that I am subject to backup withholding as a result of a failure to report all interest or dividends; or c) the IRS has notified me that I am no longer subject to backup withholding. You must cross out item 2 if you have been notified by the IRS that you are currently subject to backup withholding because of under reporting interest or dividends on your tax return.

Except as described above, we will not release information about you to others unless you or a representative whom you have authorized in writing have consented or asked us to do so, or we are required by law or other regulatory authority.

The Internal Revenue Service does not require your consent to any provision of this document other than the certification required to avoid backup withholding.

Investment Direction: Until such time as I change or revoke the designation, I hereby instruct the Record Keeper to follow the investment directions which I provide regarding the investing and reinvesting the principal and interest, as confirmed by direction letters to the record keeper from the undersigned, for the above-referenced Account or other account for which Record keeper serves as record keeper. You are authorized to accept written direction and/or verbal direction which is subsequently confirmed in writing by the authorized party, Record Keeper, or by the undersigned. Written direction shall be construed so as to include facsimile signature.

The account is established for the exclusive benefit of the Account holder or his/her beneficiaries. In taking action based on this authorization, Record Keeper may act solely on the written instruction, designation or representation of the Account holder. I expressly certify that I take complete responsibility for the type of investment instrument(s) with which I choose to fund my Account. I agree to release, indemnify, defend and hold the Record Keeper harmless from any claims, including, but not limited to, actions, liabilities, losses, penalties, fines and/or third party claims, arising out of my account and/or in connection with any action taken in reliance upon my written instructions, designations and representations, or in the exercise of any right, power or duty of Record Keeper, its agents or assigns. Record Keeper may deduct from the account any amounts to which they are entitled to the reimbursement under the foregoing hold harmless provision. Record Keeper has no responsibility or fiduciary role whatever related to or in connection with the account in taking any action related to any purchase, sale or exchange instructed by the undersigned or the undersigned's agents, including but not limited to suitability, compliance with any state or federal law or regulation, income or expense, or preservation of capital or income. For purposes of this paragraph, the term Record Keeper includes Mountain West IRA, Inc., its agents, assigns, joint ventures, licensees, franchises, affiliates and/or business partners.

In the event of claims by others related to my account and/or investment wherein Record Keeper is named as a party, Record Keeper shall have the full and

unequivocal right at their sole discretion to select their own attorneys to represent them in such litigation and deduct from my account any amounts to pay for any costs and expenses, including, but not limited to, all attorneys' fees and costs and internal costs (collectively "Litigation Costs"), incurred by Record Keeper in the defense of such claims and/or litigation. If there are insufficient funds in my account to cover the Litigation Costs incurred by Record Keeper, on demand by Record Keeper, I will promptly reimburse Record Keeper the outstanding balance of the Litigation Costs. If I fail to promptly reimburse the Litigation Costs, Record Keeper shall have the full and unequivocal right to freeze my assets, liquidate my assets, and/or initiate legal action in order to obtain full reimbursement of the Litigation Costs. I also understand and agree that the Record Keeper will not be responsible to take any action should there be any default with regard to this investment. I understand that no one at the Record Keeper has authority to agree to anything different than my foregoing understandings of the Record Keeper's policy. For purposes of this paragraph, the term Record Keeper includes Mountain West IRA, Inc., its agents, assigns, joint ventures, licensees, franchises, affiliates and/or business partners.

In executing transfers, it is understood and agreed that I will not hold Record Keeper liable or responsible for anything done or omitted in the administration, custody or investments of the account prior to the date they shall complete their respective acceptance as successor record keeper and shall be in possession of all of the assets, nor hall they have any duty or responsibility to inquire into or take any action with respect to any acts performed by the prior Custodian, or Record Keeper.

If any provision of this Application is found to be illegal, invalid, void, or unenforceable, such provisions shall be severed and such illegality or invalidity shall not affect the remaining provisions, which shall remain in full force and effect.

Important Information for Opening a New Account: To comply with the USA PATRIOT ACT, we have adopted a Customer Identification Program. All new accounts must provide a copy of an unexpired, photo-bearing, government- issued identification (e.g., driver license or passport). The copy must be readable so we can verify the client's name, driver's license number or state issued ID number. If a copy of a valid driver's license or an unexpired state issued ID card cannot be obtained, we will contact the client by telephone to verify their name, address, date of birth, and social security number.

Our Privacy Policy: You have chosen to do business with the Custodian and administrator named on your account application. As our client, the privacy of your personal non-public information is very important. We value our customer relationships and we want you to understand the protections we provide in regard to your accounts with us.

Information We May Collect: We collect non-public personal information about you from the following sources to conduct business with you:
   • Information we receive from you on applications or other forms;
   • Information about your transactions with us, or others;
Non-public personal information is non-public information about you that we may obtain in connection with providing financial products or services to you. This could include information you give us from account applications, account balances, and account history.

Information We May Share: We do not sell or disclose any non-public information about you to anyone, except as permitted by law or as specifically authorized by you. We do not share non-public personal information with our affiliates or other providers without prior approval by you. Federal law allows us to share information with providers that process and service your accounts. All providers of services in connection with the Custodian and administrator have agreed to the Custodian and administrator's confidentiality and security policies. If you decide to close your account(s) or become an inactive customer, we will adhere to the privacy policies and practices as described in this notice.

Confidentiality and Security: We restrict access to non-public personal information to those employees who need to know that information to provide products and services to you. We maintain physical, electronic, and procedural guidelines that comply with federal standards to guard your non-public personal information. The Custodian reserves the right to revise this notice and will notify you of any changes in advance.

If you have any questions regarding this policy, please contact us at the address and or telephone number listed on this application.

Signatures

As the employer, I acknowledge that I have received and reviewed a copy of the Plan and Trust document, Adoption Agreement, Employer Sponsored Plan Account Agreement, and Fee Schedule. If I am not the employer I will contact the employer who shall provide me with the appropriate information regarding my participation in this Individual(k) Plan. I understand the terms and conditions which apply to this account and are contained in this application. I agree to be bound by those terms as currently in effect or as they may be amended from time to time. I understand that failure to submit a signed Fee Schedule will result in fees "based on value of asset" (See Fee Schedule). I understand Mountain West IRA will not provide any investment advice.

Participant Signature: _____   Date: _____

MountainWest IRA *The Ultimate Retirement Machine*	**Individual(k) Plan Application**	10096 W. Fairview Ave., Ste. 160 Boise, ID 83704 Phone: (208) 377-3311 Fax: (208) 376-4567 E-Mail: accounts@MWIRA.com

Prohibited Transaction Signature Page

It is important to understand that **"You"** and **"your Qualified Plan"** are different, and your Trustee or Custodian acts on behalf of your Qualified Plan based on your direction. By inference, it is clear that "you" or any other disqualified person **can never** "buy from" or "sell to" your own Qualified Plan.

You must open a Qualified Plan, and then direct the purchase of an asset through a Direction of Investment Form. A prohibited transaction is generally defined as the improper use of your Qualified Plan by you or any disqualified person or entity.

Disqualified persons and/or entities include, but are not limited to:
- The Qualified Plan holder and his or her spouse
- The Qualified Plan holder's ancestors, lineal decedents and their spouses
- Investment advisors or managers
- Any corporation, partnership, trust or investment in which the Qualified Plan holder already has a 50% or greater interest
- Anyone providing services to the Qualified Plan such as the Trustee or Custodian
- Your plan may NOT, directly or indirectly, buy, sell, exchange, or lease any property to or from you or a disqualified person and/or entity. This includes lending money or extending credit. Your plan cannot furnish goods, services, or facilities to you or another disqualified person and/or entity. Neither you nor another disqualified person and/or entity can transfer assets to each other or use/benefit from any assets in the plan.

For a full explanation of disqualified persons and/or entities, please read Internal Revenue Code (IRC) §4975.
(www.IRS.gov)

Prohibited transactions (self-dealing) are those transactions that violate the basic intent of your IRA or Qualified Plan. They do not impose unacceptable limitations. On the contrary, there are numerous methods which do not violate the law that can be used to meet your long term objectives, and allow you to get the most out of your plan. A complete understanding of the applicable rules is encouraged, in order that you realize all the benefits available to you in directing your Qualified Plan. Please contact an ERISA attorney or your tax advisor with questions regarding your personal situation.

Loans to IRAs:

IRC §§511-514 allow for non-recourse lending to IRAs or Qualified Plans for the purchase of real estate in IRAs or Qualified Plans:
- Loans must have no recourse against the IRA or Qualified Plan, the IRA or Qualified Plan account holder, or other disqualified persons or entities
- Loans must be made by a third party not related to the IRA or Qualified Plan account holder
- IRAs or Qualified Plans with loans on assets owned by the IRA or Qualified Plan must file a 990-T unrelated debt-financed tax return annually. This tax return is procured by the IRA or Qualified Plan owner, then signed and submitted by the IRA/Qualified Plan administrator with any taxes owed by the IRA or Qualified Plan. **Taxes due may not be paid outside the IRA or Qualified Plan.**

Please sign this document and return to Mountain West IRA, Inc. indicating that you understand these Qualified Plan Prohibited Transaction and Self-Dealing Issues.

Participant Signature _____ Date_____

Appendix B
Individual K Plan Adoption Agreement

MountainWest IRA
The Ultimate Retirement Machine

INDIVIDUAL(K) PLAN

ADOPTION AGREEMENT

10096 W. Fairview Ave., Ste. 160
Boise, ID 83704
P: (866) 377-3311 | F: (208) 376-4567

609 Court Street
Clearwater, FL 33756
P: (727) 222-4200 | F: (727) 447-4567

Mountain West IRA
The Ultimate Retirement Machine

INDIVIDUAL(K) PLAN
ADOPTION AGREEMENT

10096 W. Fairview Ave., Ste. 160
Boise, ID 83704
Phone: (208) 377-3311
Fax: (208) 376-4567

General Information

The undersigned Employer hereby adopts the Sponsor's Prototype EZ-K Profit Sharing Plan in the form of a standardized Plan, as set out in this Adoption Agreement and the Prototype Defined Contribution Plan Document #01, and agrees that the following definitions, elections, and terms shall be part of such Plan.

1. Name of Employer:_____

   Street Address:_____

   Employer: ☐ is ☐ is not part of a Controlled Group or Affiliated Service Group. If "yes", complete Attachment A.

   Name of Plan:_____

2. Phone:_____

3. Trustee/Custodian:_____

4. Type of Business Entity(check one):
   - ☐ C Corporation, Date of incorporation:_____;
   - ☐ S Corporation, Date of incorporation:_____;
   - ☐ Partnership; ☐ Sole Proprietor;
   - Other (must be a legal entity recognized under federal income tax laws):_____

5. Employer's Taxable Year:_____

6. EIN#:_____   7.   3-Digit Plan Number:_____   8.   Business Code:_____

9. Plan Administrator: ☐ Employer ☐ Other (Specify):_____

10. Sponsor_____

    Address:_____

    Phone:_____

11. Depository: ☐ N/A ☐ _____

12. This is a:

    ☐ a.   New plan with an effective date of:_____

    ☐ b.   Restatement of a plan previously adopted by the Employer with an effective date of:_____ (not earlier than 1/1/02) and an

       initial effective date of:_____.

    ☐ c.   Amendment of a plan with an effective date of:_____ and an initial effective date of:_____.

    ☐ d.   Merger, amendment and restatement of the _____ and the _____ into the

       _____. The effective date of the merger is _____. The initial effective date of the surviving plan was _____.

    ☐ e.   Restatement of the _____ effective, and a restatement of the _____ effective _____, and a merger

       of the _____ into the _____.

13. This Plan shall be governed by the laws of the state or commonwealth where the Employer's (or in the case of a corporate Trustee, such

    Trustee's) principal place of business is located unless another state or commonwealth is specified:_____

14. Loans to Participants ☐ are ☐ are not available.

15. Roth Elective Deferrals ☐ shall ☐ shall not be permitted.

Page 1 of 4

101

Mountain West IRA
The Ultimate Retirement Machine

**INDIVIDUAL(K) PLAN
ADOPTION AGREEMENT**

10096 W. Fairview Ave., Ste. 160
Boise, ID 83704
Phone: (208) 377-3311
Fax: (208) 376-4567

Overriding Language for Multiple Plans

16. (a) If the Employer maintains or ever maintained another qualified plan in which any Participant in this Plan is (or was) a Participant or could become a Participant, the Employer must complete this section.

If the Participant is covered under another qualified defined contribution plan maintained by the Employer, other than a master or prototype plan:

☐ The provisions of section 6.02 of Article VI will apply as if the other plan were a master or prototype plan.

☐ (Provide the method under which the plans will limit total annual additions to the maximum permissible amount, and will properly reduce any excess amounts in a manner that precludes employer discretion):_____

(b) The Employer wishes to add overriding language to satisfy section 416 in the case of required aggregation under multiple plans:

☐ Yes (Employer must attach overriding language, if elected.)_____

☐ No

(c) If 16(b) is elected, complete the following:

☐ (i)   Interest Rate:_____

Mortality Table:_____; or

☐ (ii)   The interest rate and mortality table specified to determine "present value" for top-heavy purposes in the defined benefit plan.

Reliance on Opinion Letter

17. The adopting Employer may rely on an opinion letter issued by the Internal Revenue Service as evidence that the Plan is qualified under §401 of the Internal Revenue Code except to the extent provided in Rev. Proc. 2005-16.

An Employer who has ever maintained or later adopts any plan (including a welfare benefit fund, as defined in §419(e) of the Code, which provides post-retirement medical benefits allocated to separate accounts for key employees as defined in §419A(d) (3) of the Code, or an individual medical account as defined in §415(l) (2) of the Code) in addition to this Plan may not rely on the opinion letter issued by the Internal Revenue Service with respect to the requirements of §415 and 416.
If the Employer who adopts or maintains multiple plans wishes to obtain reliance with respect to the requirements of §415 and 416, application for a determination letter must be made to Employee Plans Determinations of the Internal Revenue Service.

The Employer may not rely on the opinion letter in certain other circumstances, which are specified in the opinion letter issued with respect to the plan or in Rev. Proc. 2005-16.

This Adoption Agreement may be used only in conjunction with basic Plan Document #1.

The Sponsor will inform the adopting Employer of any amendments it makes to the Plan or of its discontinuance or abandonment of the Plan.

NOTICE: Failure to properly complete this Adoption Agreement may result in disqualification of the Plan. The Employer's tax advisor should review the Plan and Trust and this Adoption Agreement prior to the Employer adopting such plan.

The undersigned Employer acknowledges receipt of a copy of the Plan, Trust Agreement and this Adoption Agreement on the date indicated below.

Signatures

Name of Employer:_____

Authorized Signature:_____   Date:_____

Print Name/Title of Signer:_____

Name of Trustee:_____

Authorized Signature:_____   Date:_____

Print Name/Title of Signer:_____

Plan Defaults for Profit-Sharing Plan – Plan #01007

1. The Plan Year shall be the calendar year.
2. The Limitation Year shall be the calendar year.
3. The Valuation Date shall be the last day of the Plan Year.
4. Employees who have attained the age of 21 and have completed 1 Year of Service are eligible to participate in the Plan. However, these eligibility requirements shall be waived for employees employed on the effective date of the Plan.
5. All Employees shall be eligible except the following: All Employees included in a unit of Employees covered by a collective bargaining agreement as described in Section 14.07 of the Plan; Employees who are nonresident aliens as described in Section 14.24 of the Plan; and Employees who become Employees as a result of "§410(b)(6)(C) transaction" shall not be eligible to participate in this Plan. Employees excluded as a result of a "§410(b)(6)(C) transaction" will be excluded during the period beginning on the date of the transaction and ending on the last day of the first Plan Year following the date of the transaction. A "§410(b)(6)(C) transaction" is an asset or stock acquisition, merger, or similar transaction involving a change in the Employer of the Employees of a trade or business.
6. Service under the Plan shall be computed on the basis of actual hours for which an Employee is paid or entitled to payment. A Year of Service shall mean a 12-consecutive month period during which an Employee completes at least 1000 Hours of Service. A Break in Service shall mean a 12-consecutive month period during which an Employee does not complete more than 500 Hours of Service. Contributions will be allocated to the account of each Participant regardless of the number of hours of service completed in a Plan Year. The contribution is not dependent on the Participant being employed on the last day of the Plan Year.
7. Entry Date for an eligible Employee who has completed the eligibility requirements will be the 1st day of the 1st month or the 1st day of the 7th month of the Plan Year after the Employee satisfies the eligibility requirements.
8. Vesting for all contributions under the Plan shall be full and immediate.
9. Compensation for any Participant shall be the 415 safe harbor definition as described in Section 14.38 of the Plan. Such Compensation includes such amounts that are actually paid to the Participant during the Plan Year and includes employer contributions made pursuant to a salary reduction agreement which are not includible in the gross income of the Employee under sections §§125, 132(f)(4), 402(e)(3), 402(h)(1)(b) or 403(b) of the Code. For purposes of Article VI, the preceding sentence does not apply.
10. In-service distributions are available. Once an Employee has participated in the Plan for 60 months, non-elective contributions are available for withdrawal. Prior to the 60-month period, Employees may withdraw non-elective contributions which have been in the Plan for a period of 24 months or apply for a hardship distribution. In-service distributions from non-elective contributions are available upon the Participant's attainment of age 55. Elective deferrals are available for distribution upon attainment of age 59 ½ or due to financial hardship.
11. A Participant may not elect benefits in the form of a life annuity. All forms of benefit payments are available. Benefits are available to the Participant on such Participant's termination of employment
12. The Plan is designed to operate as if it were Top-Heavy at all times.
13. The Normal Retirement Age under the Plan shall be 55.
14. The Required Beginning Date of a Participant with respect to the Plan is April 1 of the calendar year following the calendar year in which the Participant attains age 70 ½, except benefit distributions to a Participant (other than a 5-percent owner) with respect to benefits accrued after the later of the adoption or effective date of the amendment to the Plan must commence by the later of the April 1 of the calendar year following the calendar year in which the Participant attains age 70 ½ or retires.
15. Rollover and Transfer Contributions are permitted.
16. Employee Non-Deductible and Mandatory Contributions are not permitted.
17. Elective Deferrals are permitted up to the maximum permitted under §402(g) of the Code. Each participant shall have an effective opportunity to make or change an election to make Elective Deferrals (including Designated Roth Contributions) at least once each Plan Year.
18. Catch-up Contributions are permitted.

EGTRRA RESTATEMENT EFFECTIVE DATES

Note: If this plan is not a restatement of any existing Plan, this item does not apply.

General Restatement Effective Dates (If applicable enter the item number):

Provision		Effective Date
☐ a)	Not applicable. This is not an amendment and restatement.	_____
☐ b)	The eligibility requirements under Plan Defaults	_____
☐ c)	The Employer Profit Sharing contribution provisions under Plan Defaults	_____
☐ d)	The Vesting Formula under Plan Defaults	_____
☐ e)	In-Service Distributions under Plan Defaults	_____
☐ f)	Definition of Required Beginning Date under Plan Defaults	_____
☐ g)	Enter Provision and Item Number, if applicable:	_____
☐ h)	Enter Provision and Item Number, if applicable:	_____
☐ i)	Enter Provision and Item Number, if applicable:	_____

Note: The effective date(s) above may not be earlier than January 1, 2002 and not later than the last day of the Plan Year in which the Adoption Agreement is signed.

ATTACHMENT A

Name of Employer: _____

☐ Controlled Group; or ☐ Affiliated Service Group

List all "affiliated" employers with the above listed Employer.

Name	Address	EIN
1.		
2.		
3.		
4.		
5.		
6		
7.		
8.		
9.		
10.		

Appendix C
Individual K Plan and Trust Agreement

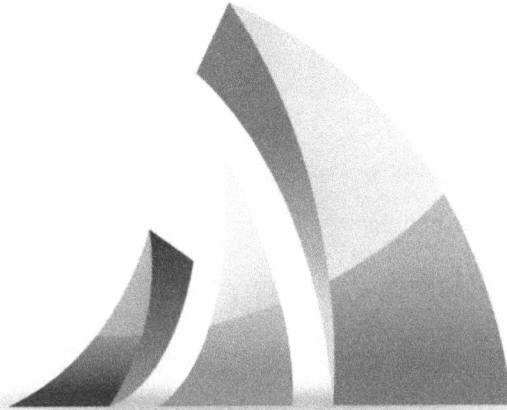

MountainWest IRA
The Ultimate Retirement Machine

INDIVIDUAL(K) PLAN

TRUST AGREEMENT

10096 W. Fairview Ave., Ste. 160
Boise, ID 83704
P: (866) 377-3311|F: (208) 376-4567

609 Court Street
Clearwater, FL 33756
P: (727) 222-4200|F: (727) 447-4567

The Mountain West IRA Individual (K) Plan Trust Agreement is a 51-page document that establishes the trust. A trust is a structure in which legal title property is transferred from the owner (the "settlor") to another party (the "trustee"), who will then administer the property for the benefit of a third party (the "beneficiary").

Mountain West IRA's trust agreement is divided into the terms of the trust and the trust agreement. The terms of the trust are as follows:

Article I – Purpose

Article II – Eligibility and Participation

Article III - Employer Contributions

Article IV – Employee Contributions

Article V – Vesting and Forfeitures

Article VI – Limitations on Allocations

Article VII – Administration of Plan

Article VIII – Top Heavy Provisions

Article IX – Joint and Survivor Annuity Requirements

Article X – Payment of Benefits

Article XI – Miscellaneous Plan Provisions

Article XII – Amendment and Termination of Plan

Article XIII – Miscellaneous Provisions

Article XIV – Glossary of Plan Terms

Article XV – Provisions for Traditional Cash or Deferred Arrangements

Article XVI – Safe Harbor Coda

Article XVII – Loans to Participants

Article XVIII – Insurance Provisions

The trust agreement is as follows:

Article 1 – Establishment of Trust

Article 2 – Investment of the Trust Fund

Article 3 – Duties of the Trustee

Article 4 – Administrative Provisions

Article 5 – Resignation and Removal of Trustee

Article 6 – No Alienation or Diversion

Article 7 – Miscellaneous Provisions

Appendix D
Transfer & Rollover Forms

Mountain West IRA The Ultimate Retirement Machine	**TRANSFER FORM** GENERAL INFORMATION (Do not use this form for a conversion to a Roth IRA)	10096 W. Fairview Ave., Ste. 160 Boise, ID 83704 Phone: (208) 377-3311 Fax: (208) 376-4567

Participant: _____ SSN: _____ Account No: _____

Address: _____ Phone: _____

Transfer Instructions

Use this form to move assets directly from one custodian to another custodian without taking receipt of the funds.
* Please do not use this form to initiate a direct rollover.

If you wish to liquidate any assets as a part of your transfer to Mountain West IRA, Inc., ensure that the liquidation process is completed PRIOR to completing this form. Otherwise, the transfer of your funds may be delayed.

Directly transfer all or part of my present retirement account with your organization in the manner indicated below.

☐ CHECK:
- Please make a check payable as follows:
  MWIRA Trust FBO (client name) IRA
- Please mail to:
  Mountain West IRA, Inc.
  10096 W. Fairview Ave., Ste. 160
  Boise, ID 83704
- Please allow 5 business days for check to clear

☐ WIRE:
If wire is requested, delivery instructions are attached ($25 Incoming wire fee applies)

2.	**Current Custodian/Trustee**
	(Where your funds are currently held)

Name of Custodian/Trustee: _____ Account Number: _____

Office Address: _____

City, State, ZIP: _____

Phone Number: _____ Contact Name: _____

3. Type of account to be transferred/eligibility *(Must transfer to the same type of account at Mountain West IRA, Inc.)*

I am transferring FROM the following type of plan: (Check one)

☐ Traditional ☐ Roth ☐ Beneficiary IRA ☐ SEP ☐ SIMPLE

☐ Other (401(k), PS, DB, 403(b). 457): _____

I am transferring TO the following type of plan: (Check one)

☐ Traditional ☐ Roth ☐ Beneficiary IRA ☐ SEP ☐ SIMPLE

☐ Other (401(k), PS, DB, 403(b). 457): _____

I am an eligible person to perform this transaction (Select One): ☐ Responsible Individual ☐ IRA holder ☐ Beneficiary of account

4. Type of asset to be transferred (Indicate whether this is **A. COMPLETE Transfer OR B. PARTIAL Transfer**)

☐ A. **COMPLETE TRANSFER to my self-directed account.** Please indicate what you would like to transfer by selecting 1) Cash AND/OR 2) In-Kind Transfer. IMPORTANT: If you need to liquidate investments, please contact the resigning Custodian and inquire about their liquidation/transfer process prior to submitting this completed form. Mountain West IRA, Inc. is not authorized to liquidate assets or investments with the resigning Custodian. (Attach your most recent statements from your prior trustee or custodian and a clear copy of a photo ID).

☐ a. **CASH*:** Send cash to **MWIRA TRUST FBO (my name)**
☐ b. **IN-KIND TRANSFER:** Transfer assets IN-KIND described below (Private Stock, Real Estate, LLCs, Notes, etc.) to: **Mountain West IRA, Inc. FBO (my name) IRA.** The term "in-kind" refers to the re-registration of an investment, etc.

☐ B. **PARTIAL TRANSFER to my self-directed account.** Please indicate what you would like transferred by selecting 1) Cash, AND/OR 2) In-Kind Transfer IMPORTANT: If you need to liquidate investments, please contact the resigning Custodian and inquire about their liquidation/transfer process prior to submitting this completed form Mountain West IRA, Inc. is not authorized to liquidate assets or investments with the resigning Custodian. (Attach your most recent statements from your prior trustee or custodian and a clear copy of a photo ID).

☐ a. **CASH*:** Send $ _____ in cash to **MWIRA TRUST FBO (my name)**
☐ b. **IN-KIND TRANSFER:** Transfer assets IN-KIND described below (Private Stock, Real Estate, LLCs, Notes, etc.) **to: Mountain West IRA, Inc. FBO (my name) IRA.** The term "in-kind" refers to the re-registration of an investment, etc.

(NOTE: A SIMPLE IRA may only be transferred to another SIMPLE IRA. After you have participated in your employer's SIMPLE plan for 2 years, you may transfer from a SIMPLE IRA to any IRA other than a Roth IRA or may convert it to a Roth IRA.)

TRANSFER FORM

5. Description of assets to be transferred (OTHER THAN CASH):

Asset Description: (DO NOT ADD CASH AMOUNT)	Amount: (DO NOT USE PERCENTAGES)

6. Delivery Instructions

a. How would you like us to send this transfer request to your current resigning Custodian?

VIA: ☐ Mail ☐ Express Delivery ($35 fee) ☐ Fax Number:_____
(Please contact your current Custodian/Trustee to verify fax number)

b. If you have selected express services above, how would you like to pay for those services?

VIA: ☐ Check ☐ Credit Card ☐ From Account

7. Signature and Acknowledgement

Signature and Acknowledgement (This does not constitute a direct rollover.)

1. I hereby agree to the terms and conditions set forth in the Account Asset Transfer Authorization and acknowledge having established a self-directed account through the execution of the _____ (type of plan) account application.

2. I understand the rules and conditions applicable to an Account Transfer.

3. I qualify for the account transfer of assets listed in the Asset Liquidation above and authorize such transactions.

4. I understand that no one at Mountain West IRA, Inc. has authority to agree to anything different than my foregoing understandings of Mountain West IRA, Inc. policy.

Participant's Signature: _____

Date: _____

(Medallion Signature Guarantee Stamp)

- **A Medallion Signature Guarantee can be obtained from your bank**
- **A notary public CANNOT provide a Medallion Signature Guarantee**
- **If your current custodian does not require a Medallion Signature Guarantee, you can simply sign and date this form**

Acceptance of Receiving Custodian

Pursuant to a limited written delegation, Mainstar Trust, as Custodian ("Custodian"), has authorized Mountain West IRA, Inc. to sign this form on the Custodian's behalf to verify the Custodian's acceptance of the transfer, rollover or direct rollover described above and agreement to apply the proceeds upon their receipt to the Account established by Mountain West IRA, Inc., on your behalf. Mainstar Trust ASSUMES NO TRUST OR FIDUCIARY OBLIGATIONS TO YOU AS IT HAS NO INVESTMENT CONTROL OVER YOUR FUNDS AND ACTS ONLY AS A CUSTODIAN OF YOUR FUNDS.

Mountain West IRA, Inc. on behalf of Custodian, Mainstar Trust.

By:_____
Lisa Galane, President, Authorized Signer

Date:_____

Account #:_____

Appendix E
Direction of Investment -- Private Placement

Mountain West IRA
The Ultimate Retirement Machine

**DIRECTION OF INVESTMENT
PRIVATE PLACEMENT**

10096 W. Fairview Ave., Ste. 160
Boise, ID 83704
Phone: (208) 377-3311
Fax: (208) 376-4567

Note: All investment paperwork must be titled in the name of your account. For example:
"Mountain West IRA, Inc. FBO (Account Holder's Name) IRA"
If you have a 401(k) account, please call our office for correct vesting.

A: ACCOUNT INFORMATION

Your Name: _____ Account No.: _____
Address: _____
SSN: _____ Birth Date: _____ Phone: _____

B: HOW WOULD YOU LIKE TO PAY YOUR FEES?
(All fees are due prior to funding)

Choose one:
☐ My Account   ☐ Credit Card on File
☐ Check Enclosed   ☐ Credit Card Authorization Form Attached

C: FUNDING INSTRUCTIONS

Make Payable to: _____

Address: _____

City: _____ State: _____ ZIP: _____

Sent By:
☐ Wire (attach wire instructions)   ☐ Regular Mail
☐ Check   ☐ Overnight Mail
☐ Cashier's Check   ☐ Will Pick Up

D: INVESTMENT DETAILS

D1.   ☐ New Private Entity Investment   ☐ Additional Funding Investment

D2. Name of Private Entity: _____   D3. EIN of Private Entity: _____

D4. Quantity: (number of shares, units, etc.)	D5. Price (per share, unit, etc.)	D6. Total Purchase Price (Quantity x Price)

D7. Will this investment have multiple capital calls? ☐ Yes   ☐ No (If yes, complete Special Instructions)

D8. Special Instructions:

D9.

Total: $_____

D10. ☐ I have signed and submitted the Private Placement Disclaimer & Indemnity Agreement

D11. ☐ I have signed and submitted the Private Placement Instruction Letter

D12. Have you completed your due diligence on this investment?   ☐ YES   ☐ NO

MountainWest IRA
The Ultimate Retirement Machine

DIRECTION OF INVESTMENT
PRIVATE PLACEMENT

10096 W. Fairview Ave., Ste. 160
Boise, ID 83704
Phone: (208) 377-3311
Fax: (208) 376-4567

AUTHORIZATION

I confirm that I am directing Mountain West IRA, Inc., Administrator, to complete this transaction as specified above. I understand that my account is self-directed, and I take complete responsibility for any investment I choose for my account, including the investment specified in this Direction of Investment. I understand that neither the Administrator nor the Custodian (Mainstar Trust) sells or endorses any investment products, and that they are not affiliated in any way with any investment provider. I understand that the roles of Administrator and Custodian are limited, and their responsibilities do not include investment selection for my account. I acknowledge that neither the Administrator nor the Custodian has provided or assumed responsibility for any tax, legal, or investment advice with respect to this investment, and I agree that they will not be liable for any loss which results from my decision to purchase the investment. I understand that neither the Administrator nor the Custodian has reviewed or will review the merits, legitimacy, appropriateness or suitability of this investment, and I certify that I have done my own due diligence investigation prior to instructing the Administrator to make this investment for my account. I understand that neither the Administrator nor the Custodian determines whether this investment is acceptable under the Employee Retirement securities Income Act (ERISA), the Internal Revenue Code (IRC), or any applicable federal, state, or local laws, including securities laws. I understand that it is my responsibility to review any investments to ensure compliance with the requirements.

I understand that in processing the transaction the Administrator and the Custodian are only acting as my agent, and nothing will be construed as conferring fiduciary status on either the Administrator or the Custodian. I agree that the Administrator and the Custodian will not be liable for any investment losses sustained by me or my account as a result of this transaction. I agree to indemnify and hold harmless the Administrator and the Custodian from any and all claims, damages, liability, actions, costs, expenses (including reasonable attorneys' fees) and any loss to my account as a result of any action taken in connection with this investment transaction or resulting from serving as the Administrator or the Custodian for this investment, including, without limitation, claims, damages, liability, actions, and losses asserted by me.

I understand that if this Direction of Investment and any accompanying documentation are not received as required, or, if received, are unclear in the opinion of the Administrator, or if there is insufficient Undirected Cash in my account to fully comply with my instructions to purchase the investment and to pay all fees, the Administrator may not process this transaction until proper documentation and/or clarification is received, and the Administrator will have no liability for loss of income or appreciation.

I understand that my account is subject to the provisions of Internal Revenue Code (IRC) §4975, which defines certain prohibited transactions. I acknowledge that neither the Administrator nor the Custodian has made or will make any determination as to whether this investment is prohibited under §4975 or under any other federal, state or local law. I certify that making this investment will not constitute a prohibited transaction and that it complies with all application federal, state, and local laws, regulations, and requirements.

I understand that my account is subject to the provisions of IRC §§511-514 relating to Unrelated Business Taxable Income (UBTI) of tax-exempt organizations. If this investment generates UBTI, I understand that I will be responsible for preparing or having prepared the required IRS Form 990-T tax return and any other documents that may be required. I understand that neither the Administrator nor the Custodian makes any determination of whether or not investments in my account generate UBTI.

I understand that the assets in my account are required by the IRS to be valued annually as of the end of each calendar year. I agree to provide the prior year end value of this investment by no later than January 10th of each year on a form provided by the Administrator, with substantiation attached to support the value provided.

I understand that with some types of accounts there are rules for Required Minimum Distributions (RMDs) from the account. If I am now subject to the RMD rules in my account, or if I will become subject to those rules during the term of this investment, I represent that I have verified either that the investment will provide income or distributions sufficient to cover each RMD, or that there are assets in my account or in other accounts that are sufficiently liquid (including cash) from which I will be able to withdraw my RMDs. I understand that failure to take RMDs may result in a tax penalty of 50% of the amount I should have withdrawn.

I understand that all communication regarding this transaction must be in writing and must be signed by me or by my authorized agent on my behalf, and that no oral communication of my instructions will be valid.

I understand that neither the Administrator nor the Custodian bears or assumes any responsibility to notify me to secure or maintain any fire, casualty, liability or other insurance coverage, including but not limited to title insurance coverage, on this investment or on any property which serves as collateral for this investment. I acknowledge and agree that it is my sole responsibility to decide what insurance is necessary or appropriate for investments in my account, and to direct the Administrator in writing (on a form prescribed by the Administrator) to pay the premiums for any such insurance.

I further understand that neither the Administrator nor the Custodian is responsible for notification or payment of any real estate taxes, homeowners association dues, utilities or other charges with respect to this investment unless I specifically direct the Administrator to pay these amounts in writing (on a form prescribed by the Administrator), and sufficient funds are available to pay these amounts from my account. I acknowledge that it is my responsibility to provide to the Administrator or to ensure that the Administrator has received any and all bills for insurance, taxes, homeowner's dues, utilities or other amounts dues for this investment. Furthermore, I agree that it is my responsibility to determine that payments have been made by reviewing my account statements.

I understand that no person at the office of the Administrator or the Custodian has the authority to modify any of the foregoing provisions. I certify that I have examined the Direction of Investment and any accompanying documents or information, and to the best of my knowledge and belief, it is all true, correct, and complete.

AUTHORIZED BY (check one):

☐ Account Holder

☐ Limited Power of Attorney

_____   _____
Signature   Date

Appendix F
Unrelated Debt-Financed Income Procedures
Unrelated Debt Financed Income Procedures

Computation of Debt-Financed Income: IRC 512(b)(4) provides that an organization subject to IRC 511 must include any gross income from an unrelated trade or business, unrelated debt-financed income. For each debt-financed property, the unrelated debt-financed income is that amount which is the same percentage (not over 100 percent) of the total gross income derived during a taxable year from such property as the average acquisition indebtedness regarding the property is of the average adjusted basis of the property. This percentage is referred to in Reg. 1.514(a)-1(a)(1)(iii) as the debt/basis percentage.

The term *average acquisition indebtedness* means the amount of outstanding principal indebtedness during that portion of the taxable year the property is held by an organization. Average acquisition indebtedness is computed by determining principal indebtedness on the first day of each calendar month during the taxable year, adding them together, and then dividing the sum by the total number of months during the year the organization held the property. A fractional part of a month is treated as a full month in computing average acquisition indebtedness. Reg. 1.514(a)-1(a)(3)(ii).

The average adjusted basis of debt-financed property is the average amount of the adjusted basis of such property during that portion of the taxable year it is held by an organization. It is computed by averaging the adjusted basis as of the first day and as of the last day during the taxable year that the organization holds the property. (See IRC 1011 and the Regulations thereunder to determine the adjusted basis of property).

The deductions allowable are those items allowed as deductions by Chapter 1 of the Code which are directly connected with the debt-financed property or income therefrom except that (a) the allowable deductions are subject to the modifications provided by IRC 512(b) on computation of the unrelated business taxable income, and (b) the depreciation deduction under IRC 167 is computed only by use of the straight-line method. Reg.

1.514(a)-1(b)(2). To be directly connected with debt-financed property or the income therefrom, an item of deduction must have proximate or primary relationship to such property or incomes. Expenses, depreciation, and similar items attributable solely to such property qualify for deduction to the extent they meet the above requirements.

Example: If the straight-line depreciation allowance for an office building is $10,000 a year, an organization would be allowed a deduction for depreciation of $10,000 if the entire building were debt-financed property. However, if only half of the building were treated as debt-financed property, the depreciation allowed as a deduction would be $5,000.

Under IRC 514(a)(2), the deductions allowed with respect to each debt-financed property are determined by applying the debt/basis percentage to the sum of the deductions allowed. The formulas for deriving unrelated debt-financed income are:

1. Average Acquisition Indebtedness/Average Acquisition Basis= Debt/Basis %

2. Debt/Basis % x Gross Income from Debt-Financed Property= UFDI

Under this formula, the percentage of income treated as income from an unrelated trade or business decreases as the indebtedness on the debt-financed property decreases.

Example: X, an SDIRA, owns an office building which is debt-financed property. The building in 2010 produces $10,000 of gross rental income. The Average Adjusted Basis of the building for 2010 is $100,000, and the Average Acquisition Indebtedness with respect to the building in 2010 is $50,000. Accordingly, the Debt/Basis Percentage for 2010 is 50 percent (the ratio of $50,000 to $100,000). Therefore, the Unrelated Debt-Financed Income with respect to the building for 2010 is $5,000 (50 percent of $10,000).

If, after applying the Debt/Basis Percentage to the income and deductions from Debt-Financed property, the deductions exceed such income, the SDIRA has a net operating loss for the tax- able year. This amount may be carried back or forward to other taxable years in

115

accordance with IRC 512(b)(6). However, the Debt/Basis Percentage is not applied in such other taxable years to determine the amounts that may be taken as deductions in those years. Reg. 1.514(a)-l(b)(5).

Example: A property is debt-financed property. During 2010, Y an SDIRA, receives $20,000 of rent from a building which it owns. Y has no other Unrelated Business Taxable Income for 2010. For 2010, the deductions directly connected with this building are property taxes of $5,000, interest of $5,000 on the acquisition indebtedness, and salary of $15,000 to the manager of the building. The Debt/Basis Percentage of 2010 with respect to the building is 50 percent. Under these circumstances, Y must take into account in computing its Unrelated Business Taxable Income for 2010, $10,000 of income (50 percent of $20,000) and $12,500 (50 percent of $25,000) of the deductions directly connected with such income. Thus, for 2010, Y has sustained a net operating loss of $2,500 ($10,000 of income less $12,500 of deductions) which may be carried back or carried over to other taxable years without further application of the Debt/Basis Percentage.

If an organization sells or otherwise disposes of Debt-Financed Property, it must include in computing Unrelated Business Taxable Income an amount with respect to any gain (or loss) which is the same percentage (not over 100 percent) of the total gain (or loss) derived from the sale as (a) the highest Acquisition Indebtedness regarding the property during the 12-month period preceding the date of disposition is of (b) the Average Adjusted Basis of such property. Reg. 1.514(a)-1(a) (1) (v) (b) provides that the tax on this amount is determined in accordance with the rules regarding capital gains and losses. (Subchapter P, Chapter 1 of the Code).

If the sale or exchange of debt-financed property results in a capital loss, the amount of such loss taken into account in the taxable year in which the loss arises is computed in determining the gain (or loss) from the sale or other disposition of the property. If any part of the loss may be carried back, or forward to another taxable year, it is taken as a

116

deduction for that year without further application of the Debt/Basis Percentage for such year.

The calculation of gain on the sale must also take into account depreciation recapture and any suspended loss carry-forward. Depreciation is a decreased or loss in value due to age, wear or market conditions. For accounting purposes, the IRS permits an allowance to be deducted as an expense for the loss in value of the property. This expense reduces net income. When a property is sold, the IRS requires that any depreciation taken over the life of the asset be recaptured and a tax assessed of 25 percent against the depreciation recapture. It is, therefore, necessary when computing gain on the sale to determine both the actual amount of the depreciation recapture and the amount of net gain on the sale. Depreciation recapture is taxed at 25 percent and the remaining capital gain is taxed at 15 percent, if the asset has been held for more than a year. If the property had suspended loss carry-forward, which means that all of the depreciation write off and other expenses contributing to the loss could not be offset against income and was therefore carried-forward, must also be taken into consideration prior to calculating the taxes due on the gain.

Calculation of the gain on the sale and the taxes clue, is further complicated when the asset is purchased using self-directed IRA funds and the property has debt. Neither the depreciation recapture nor capital is relevant for the percentage of the property that was purchased with IRA funds. Only that portion of the property that was attributable to the debt financing is relevant for the computation of taxes due on the sale. Therefore, once the capital gain has been determined it must be reduced by the percentage of the property that was financed with IRA funds, prior to calculating depreciation recapture and capital gains. The case study illustrates how depreciation recapture and capital gain is applied to the sale of a property.

Case Study

This case study applies the procedures mentioned above in the section entitled, Special Considerations When Buying Real Estate, to an actual property that is purchased using Self-Directed IRA funds and debt financing. Determination of the Internal Rate of Return is illustrated step-by-step starting with the acquisition of the property to the disposition of the property.

STEP 1 - Determine the Acquisition Cost. For this illustration, the acquisition cost is as follows:

Category	Cost	Percent of Total Cost
Land Cost	$360,000	30%
Development Cost	$60,000	5%
Construction Cost	$600,000	50%
Soft Costs	$120,000	10%
Profit	$60,000	5%
Total Costs	$1,200,000	100%

STEP 2 - Determine the Loan Amount. Term of the loan is 30 years at 7% interest.

Category	Amount	Percent of Total Cost
Equity Contribution	$240,000	20%
Loan Amount	$960,000	80%
Total Amount	$1,200,000	100%

STEP 3 - Determine the Holding Period. For this illustration, the Holding Period is 5 years.

STEP 4 - Determine the Annual Gross Income.

	Year 1	Year 2	Year 3	Year 4	Year 5
Revenue	$105,000	$105,000	$105,000	$105,000	$105,000
Operating Expenses	$5,250	$5,250	$5,250	$5.250	$5,250
Net Operating Income	$ 99,750	$ 99,750	$ 99,750	$99,750	$ 99,750

STEP 5 - Calculate Depreciation using the Cost Segregation/Straight Line Method.

Acquisition Cost	$1,200,000
Less Land Cost	$ 360,000
Depreciable Value	$ 840,000
Depreciation	
Year 1	$ 25,890
Year2	$ 44,806

Year 3	$ 36,528
Year 4	$ 30,583
Year 5	$ 26,605
Total	$ 164,512

STEP 6 - Amortize the loan over the Holding Period.

	Beginning Balance	Loan Payment	Interest	Principal	Remaining Balance
Year 1	$960,000	$76,643	$66,891	$9,752	$950,248
Year 2	950,248	$76,643	$66,186	$10,457	$939,792
Year 3	$939,792	$76,643	$65,430	$11,213	$928,579
Year 4	$928,579	$76,643	$64,620	$12,023	$916,556
Year 5	$916,556	$76,643	$63,750	$12,892	$903,664

STEP 7 - Deduct Allowable Expenses from Gross Income to determine Net Income.

	Year 1	Year 2	Year 3	Year4	Year 5
Revenue	$105,000	$105,000	$105,000	$105,000	$105,000
Operating Expenses	$5,250	$5,250	$5,250	$5,250	$5,250
Net Operating Income	$ 99,750	$ 99,750	$ 99,750	$ 99,750	$ 99,750
Interest	$66,891	$66,186	$65,430	$64,620	$63,750
Depreciation	$25,890	$44,806	$36,528	$30,583	$26,605
Net Income/Loss	$7,169	-$11,242	-$2,108	$4,547	$9,395

STEP 8 - Determine Net Loss Carryforward, if any. For example, Year 2 above has a Net Loss of $11,242. That Net Loss would be carried-forward to Year 3, Year 4 and so on when calculating the Unrelated Debt Financed Income.

STEP 9 - Calculate the Average Acquisition Indebtedness.

	Year 1	Year2	Year 3	Year 4	Year 5
Month 1	959,213	949,404	938,887	927,609	915,516
Month 2	958,422	948,556	937,977	926,633	914,469
Month 3	957,626	947,702	937,061	925,651	913,417
Month 4	956,825	946,843	936,141	924,664	912,358
Month 5	956,019	945,980	935,215	923,671	911,293
Month 6	955,209	945,111	934,283	922,672	910,222
Month 7	954,394	944,237	933,346	921,668	909,145
Month 8	953,575	943,359	932,404	920,657	908,061
Month 9	952,750	942,475	931,456	919,641	906,971
Month 10	951,921	941,585	930,503	918,618	905,875
Month 11	951,087	940,691	929,544	917,590	904,773
Month 12	950,248	939,792	928,579	916,556	906,664
Average	954,774	944,645	933,783	922,136	909,897

STEP 10 - Calculate the Average Adjusted Basis.

	Year 1	Year 2	Year 3	Year 4	Year 5
Beginning Basis	1,200,000	1,174,310	1,129,504	1,092,976	1,062,393
Depreciation	25,690	44,806	36,528	30,583	26,605
Ending Basis	1,174,310	1,129,504	1,092,976	1,062,393	1,035,788
Average	1,187,155	1, 151,907	1,111,240	1,077,685	1,049,091

STEP 11 - Calculate the Debt/Basis Percentage by dividing the Average Acquisition Indebtedness by the Average Adjusted Basis.

	Year 1	Year 2	Year 3	Year 4	Year 5
Debt/Basis Percent	80.43%	82.01%	84.03%	85.57%	86.73%

STEP 12 - Multiply the Net Income/Loss by the Debt/Basis Percentage to determine the Unrelated Debt Financed Income. If the amount is below zero, use zero as the UDFI.

	Year 1	Year 2	Year 3	Year 4	Year 5
Net Income (Loss)	$15,530	-$2,969	$5,971	$12,625	$17,363
Debt/Basis Percent	70.37%	73.54%	76.24%	79.13%	82.34%
Unrelated Debt Financed Income	$10,929	-$2,183	$2,369	$9,990	$14,296

STEP 13 - Multiply the UDFI by the Trust Rate

	Year 1	Year 2	Year 3	Year 4	Year 5
Unrelated Debt Financed Income	$5,766	-$9,219	-$2,108	$3,891	$8,148
Loss Carryforward	$5,766	-$3,454	-$5,561	-$1,670	$6,478
$0 < $2,200 (15%)		$0	$0	$0	
$2,200 < $5,150 ($330 + 25%)					
$5,150 < $7,850 ($1,067.50 + 28%)	$484				$1,070
$7,850 < $10,700 ($1,823.50 + 33%)					
$10,700 > ($2,764 + 35%)					
Tax on UDFI	$484	$0	$0	$0	$1,070

STEP 14 - Determine the Suspended Loss. Suspended Losses occur if there is a Net Loss for the Holding Period. In this example, there is a Net Loss in Years 2 and 3 but it is offset by Net Income in Years 1, 4, and 5, therefore there is no Suspended Loss for the project.

STEP 15 - Determine the Annual Cash Flow.

	Year 1	Year 2	Year 3	Year 4	Year 5
Revenue	$105,000	$105,000	$105,000	$105,000	$105,000
Operating Expenses	$5,250	$5,250	$5,250	$5,250	$5,250
Net Operating Income	$ 99,750	$ 99,750	$ 99,750	$ 99,750	$ 99,750
Interest	$66,891	$66,186	$65,430	$64,620	$63,750
Depreciation	$25,890	$44,806	$36,528	$30,583	$26,605
Net Income/Loss	$7,169	-$11,242	-$2,108	$4,547	$9,395
Add back Depreciation	$25,690	$44,806	$36,828	$30,583	$26,505
Deduct Principal Pmts	$9,752	$10,457	$11,213	$12,023	$12,892
Deduct UDFI Tax	$484	$0	$0	$0	$1,070
Net Cash Flow	$22,623	$23,107	$23,1 07	$23,107	$21,708

STEP 16 - Determine the Adjusted Cost Basis by subtracting the Accumulated Depreciation from the Original Basis. (Original Basis $1,200,000-Accumulated Depreciation $164.512 = Adjusted Cost Basis of $1,035,488).

STEP 17 - Estimate the Adjusted Sales Price

	In the Year of the Sale
Revenue	$105,000
Operating Expenses	$5,250
Net Operating Income	$99,750
Capitalization Rate	7.5%
Sales Price	$1,400,000
Less Real Estate Commission	$84,000
Less Closing Costs	$25,000
Adjusted Sales Price	$1,291,000

STEP 18 - Calculate the Gain on the Sale. After the Gain on the Sale has been determined, the sum must be multiplied by the percent of the gain which is attributable to the Unrelated Debt Financed Income $255,512 x 86.73% = $221,611). This is calculated by multiplying the Gain on the Sale by the Debt/Basis Percent for the year of sale. There are two components to the Gain. The first component is Depreciation Recapture ($164,212 x 86.73% = $142,424) which is taxed at 25% and the second component is Long-term Capital Gain attributable to UDFI ($221,611 - $142,424 = $79,186) which is taxed at 15%.

	In the Year of the Sale
Adjusted Sales Price	$1,291,000
Adjusted Cost Basis	$1,035,488
Gain on Sale	$255,512
Gain Attributable to UDFI	$221,611
UDFI Depreciation Recapture	$142,424
UDFI Gain on Sale	$79,186
Tax on Recapture @ 25%	$35,606
Tax on Net Gain @ 15%	$11,878
Total Tax Due on Sale	$47,484

121

STEP 19 - Determine the Cash at Closing.

Adjusted Sales Price	$1,291,000
Mortgage Balance	$903,664
Cash at Closing	$387,336
Total Tax Due on Sale	$47,484
Net Cash at Closing	$339,852

STEP 20 - Calculate the Internal Rate of Return. The cash inflow in Year 5 is the sum of $339,852 Net Cash at Closing plus $21,708 Annual Net Cash Flow for Year 5 minus $47,484 Tax Due.

Period	Cash Outlays & Inflows	Participation @ 70%
0	-$240,000	-$240,000
1	$22,623	$15,836
2	$23,107	$16,175
3	$23,107	$16,175
4	$23,107	$16,175
5	$361,560	$326,071
Internal Rate of Return	15.59%	11.35%

Please note that the Unrelated Debt Financed Income, Depreciation Recapture and Capital Gains Tax has an impact on the Internal Rate of Return, but the return is better than if an investor used after-tax dollars to make the same real estate investment. The return is also better by using debt, even if the investor has to give up a portion of the overall cash to the partner guaranteeing the loan, than it would be if the transaction were an all cash deal. Using leverage still significantly enhances the Internal Rate of Return for the SDIRA investor.

Answer Key for Review Questions

Section One

1. A
2. C
3. B
4. B
5. A
6. D
7. B
8. C
9. A
10. D
11. C
12. A

Section Two

1. A
2. C
3. B
4. D
5. A
6. D
7. B
8. C
9. A
10. D
11. B
12. C

Section Three

1. A
2. B
3. D
4. B
5. A
6. A
7. D
8. D
9. B
10. B
11. B
12. D

Section Four

1. B
2. D
3. A
4. B
5. D
6. A
7. C
8. D
9. A
10. D
11. D
12. A

Section Five

1. A
2. B
3. C
4. C
5. D
6. D
7. C
8. B
9. C

Section Six

1. A
2. A
3. C
4. D
5. B
6. D
7. A
8. C
9. B
10. D

Section Seven

1. A
2. D
3. D
4. B
5. A
6. B
7. C
8. D
9. D
10. B